KEY THINKERS
IN THE STUDY
OF RELIGION

Lévi-Strauss on Religion

The Structuring Mind

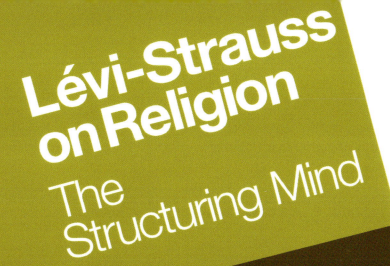

Claude Lévi-Strauss

Paul-François Tremlett

Lévi-Strauss on Religion

Key Thinkers in the Study of Religion

Edited by Steven Engler, Mount Royal College, Canada

Key Thinkers in the Study of Religion is a series of compact introductions to the life and work of major figures in the study of religion. Each volume provides up-to-date critical evaluations of the place and value of a single scholar's work, in a manner both accessible to students and useful for instructors. Each volume includes a brief biography, analyses of key works, evaluations of criticisms and of overall impact on the field, and discussions of the work of later scholars who have appropriated or extended each key thinker's approach. Critical engagement with each key thinker's major works makes each volume a useful companion for the study of these important sources in the field. Aimed at the undergraduate and introductory graduate classrooms, the series aims to encapsulate and evaluate foundational contributions to the academic study of religion.

This series is sponsored by, supported by the North American Association for the Study of Religion (NAASR), an affiliate of the International Association for the History of Religions.

Published:

Bourdieu on Religion: Imposing Faith and Legitimacy
Terry Rey

Forthcoming:

Bastide on Religion: The Invention of Candomblé
Michel Despland

Dumont on Religion: Difference, Comparison, Transgression
Ivan Strenski

Derrida on Religion
Dawne McCance

Rudolf Otto on Religion
Gregory D. Alles

Lévi-Strauss on Religion:
The Structuring Mind

Paul-François Tremlett

LONDON   OAKVILLE

Published by Equinox Publishing Ltd.

UK: Unit 6, The Village, 101 Amies St.,London SW11 2JW
USA: DBBC, 28 Main Street, Oakville, CT 06779

www.equinoxpub.com

First published 2008

British Library Cataloguing-in-Publication Data
A catalogue record for this book is available from the British Library.

Library of Congress Cataloging-in-Publication Data

Tremlett, Paul-François.
Levi-Strauss on religion / Paul-François Tremlett.
    p. cm. — (Key thinkers in the study of religion)
Includes bibliographical references and index.
ISBN-13: 978-1-84553-277-2 (hb)
ISBN-13: 978-1-84553-278-9 (pbk.)
1. Lévi-Strauss, Claude. 2. Religion. I. Title.
BL51.T635 2008
200.92—dc22
                    2008003006

Edited and Typeset by Queenston Publishing, Hamilton, Canada

Printed and bound in Great Britain by Lightning Source UK, Ltd., Milton Keynes, and Lightning Source Inc., La Vergne, TN

Contents

Preface

> The customs of a community, taken as a whole, always have a particular style and are reducible to systems. I am of the opinion that the number of such systems is not unlimited and that—in their games, dreams or wild imaginings—human societies, like individuals, never create absolutely, but merely choose certain combinations from an ideal repertoire that it should be possible to define. By making an inventory of all recorded customs, of all those imagined in myths or suggested in children's games or adult games, or in the dreams of healthy or sick individuals or in psycho-pathological behaviour, one could arrive at a sort of table, like that of the chemical elements, in which all actual or hypothetical customs would be grouped in families, so that one could see at a glance which customs a particular society had in fact adopted. (Claude Lévi-Strauss, *Tristes Tropiques*)

Three insuperable difficulties present themselves at the outset of this book whose remit lies in the critical exposition of the ideas and writings of Claude Lévi-Strauss for a religious studies—or as I prefer—a study of religions, audience. The first concerns the status of structuralism, a movement, fashion or mode of thought with which Claude Lévi-Strauss, to his liking or not, will always be associated. Structuralism appeared to promise a true and total science of humankind, a grand promise to be sure and one which proved to be, as with it seems all such promises, illusory. Among the ruins, signposts pointing to numerous allegedly devastating critiques can be found, a literature almost as daunting as Lévi-Strauss' own writings. Yet, while this book must maintain throughout a critical approach to Lévi-Strauss' equally considerable *oeuvre*, it is surely also incumbent on a book such as this to demonstrate that, however unfashionable, discredited or indeed difficult, Lévi-Strauss ranks as one of the most important thinkers of our time. As such, we ignore those writings that bear his name at our peril.

The second concerns the focus of this book on an individual thinker as an author and as an autonomous, meaning-endowing subject, possessing intentions and whose life might constitute a sure ground for establishing the truth and meaning of the texts that carry his name. Of himself Lévi-Strauss has said "I don't have the feeling that I write my books. I have the feeling that my books get written through me" (Lévi-Strauss 2001, 1). He has also stated that "analysis could never be carried very far if we felt ourselves to be bound by what the creators themselves say, or may even believe, about their works" (Lévi-Strauss 1981, 660). The irony here is the assumption that a putative author and his or her life can function as some kind of guarantee of meaning and truth is one that cuts against the grain of the manner of thinking which Lévi-Strauss and structuralism (dis) embodied. In other words, in a certain sense the writing of this book constitutes a disavowal of the philosophical, theoretical and methodological tenets with which Lévi-Strauss is associated and indeed with which I am in broad agreement.

The third concerns the nature of the supposed audience for this book. The study of religions is a field of enquiry that lacks any clear or singular definition of its object or a specific procedure, method or set of assumptions by which the study of religions might claim for itself the (dubious) status of a "discipline." The consequence of this fact is that there is no study of religions audience, only loose groupings of individuals who study religions from a variety of disciplinary, theoretical and methodological positions. Nevertheless, there is one approach, known as the phenomenology of religion that has more than any other defined debates about theory and method in the study of religions. Phenomenologists of religion—typically claiming to draw from Husserl's search for a philosophy without presuppositions—have commonly asserted that religion is a *sui generis* phenomenon and must be studied on its own terms. Religion is assumed to be an autonomous and distinct sphere of human belief and practice concerned with relating human beings to a transcendent supernatural or sacred reality. Furthermore, the phenomenologist of religion, through the invocation of the phenomenological *epoché*, avoids or rather brackets out values and judgements as to the truth or falsity of particular religious beliefs, and instead concerns him or herself first with encountering or witnessing the phenomena objectively as it appears and, secondly, with preserving the integrity of a putative believer's point of view which is to be accessed or re-experienced through intuitive or empathic liason. Finally, it is argued that, given the irreducibility of religion and therefore of the believer's point of view, the scholar of religion ought to be, usually in some vague and unspecified sense, an "insider" or at least in sympathy with the insider's point of view in order to be properly capable of representing the interiority of "the" religious commitment. However, commitment to the value-free description of "religious facts" is frequently over-written by the claim that phenomenological description should aim at manufacturing, within a putative reader, some kind of spiritual awakening (Otto 1928,12; Eliade 1969) and by value-saturated claims about "profane existence" that amount to a species of culture critique (Eliade 1959, 10–24). Religions are as such constituted as "worldviews" that demand a "special hermeneutics" and also as unique sources of knowledge that can be appropriated to enchant the world once more. We will return to the phenomenology of religion at the end of this book.

Despite such caveats and abdications, even a brief review of litera-ture pertaining to the discussion or elaboration of theory and method in the study of religions yields the following salutary observation: sustained analysis and discussion of the ideas and writings of Claude Lévi-Strauss has barely begun (Penner 1989 4, 129). This might be explained or per-haps excused by the wealth of literature, across a variety of disciplinary lines of demarcation, already dedicated to him. However, this has hardly prevented the likes of Capps (1995), Connolly (1999), Flood (1999), Ham-ilton (2001), Pals (2006), Segal (1999), Sharpe (1986) or Turner (1991), from discussing other thinkers—including anthropologists—of compa-rable eminence. There are, of course, some notable exceptions: Kunin (2003), Lawson and McCauley (1990), Penner (1989), Segal (2004) and Strenski (1987) have all written about Lévi-Strauss, though their focus has been either somewhat narrower than that which has been attempted here or directed towards answering a different set of questions and problems. Faced, then, with such an evident blind spot, a book such as this—a book which seeks to offer a critical overview of Lévi-Strauss' ideas and writings and which situates those writings in terms of current debates in the study of religions—is surely long overdue.

Paul-François Tremlett

Acknowledgements

It is only proper that I take this opportunity to thank those who, at various moments in the writing of this book, have offered comments and observations either in conversation or more directly through a critical reading of the text itself. First, I would like to thank Steven Engler, Stephan Feuchtwang, Peter Flügel, Stuart Thompson and Anna Lora-Wainwright for their helpful suggestions. Of course, all errors in fact and interpretation remain my own. Secondly, I would like to extend my thanks to Richard Bartholomew for his assistance with the index and the final formatting of the manuscript, and to Russell Adams and Valerie Hall at Equinox. Finally, I would like to dedicate this essay to my father Peter Ian Tremlett (1940–2005) whose love for books and knowledge still inspires.

Introduction

An intellectual biography

The ultimate goal of the human sciences is not to constitute, but to dissolve man. (Claude Lévi-Strauss, *The Savage Mind*)

Claude Lévi-Strauss was born on November 28, 1908 in Brussels, though soon after his parents returned to Paris where he has since lived for most of his life. During his teenage years Lévi-Strauss was introduced to the writings of Marx and Proudhon by a friend of the family through whom he became associated with the Belgian Workers Party. His first published work—on Gracchus Babeuf—was printed by the Party press, and he also became active within the French socialist party (SFIO). He was later secretary of the socialist study group of students for the five Ecoles Normales Supérieures and general secretary of the Federation of Socialist Students (Fédération des Etudiants Socialistes). He obtained a degree in philosophy from the Sorbonne and one in law from the Faculté de Droit, though he claims to have gone through the whole time "like a zombie, with the feeling I was outside it all" (Lévi-Strauss and Eribon 1991, 10).

After *aggrégation* in 1931, he was appointed to teach in the *lycée* at Mont-de-Marsan. He stayed for a year before taking a second appointment at Laon. It was at this time that he married his first wife, Dina Drey-fus. Throughout this period he continued his political activities, though by this time bored with teaching he made up his mind to become an anthro-

---

In this chapter:

- A brief biographical sketch of Lévi-Strauss' academic career.
- Synopsis of chapters outlining key topics and points of discussion and critique of Lévi-Strauss' contribution to the study of religions.
- A short section suggesting how to use this book.

---

pologist, inspired at least in part by his reading of Robert Lowie's *Primitive Society*. With the help of Célestin Bouglé who had directed his thesis and Georges Dumas, he left for Brazil in early 1935 to take a position at the then new University of São Paulo. Lévi-Strauss showed an interest in the material cultures of the Indian peoples he encountered, and he and his wife accumulated a collection of objects including costumes, weapons and ceramics which were exhibited in Paris at the Musée de l'Homme in 1937 (Deliège 2004, 8; Hénaff 1998, 248). He returned to Brazil in 1938 to conduct a fieldwork expedition. It was during this trip that Lévi-Strauss conducted field research among the Nambikwara, Bororo, Caduveo and Tupi-Kawahib. While he was in Brazil he published a number of articles though he has since claimed that these were more examples of journalism than ethnography. Indeed, Lévi-Strauss' best-known anthropological works have tended to consist of critical reviews of ethnographic materials collected by others. Lévi-Strauss' fame and influence is most certainly not based in any prowess as an ethnographer.

When he returned to France in 1939 Lévi-Strauss was drafted, though by September 1940 he was already "de-mobilized." He separated from his wife at this time. Initially and perhaps naïvely, he went to Vichy to ask to be assigned to a new teaching post. He was named Professor of Philosophy at the *lycée* in Montpellier but was dismissed three weeks later because of his Jewish ancestry. He then tried but failed to get a visa to return to Brazil, though Roger Bastide had by then stepped into his shoes at the University of São Paulo (he would not return to Brazil until 1985). At this time he read Marcel Granet's *Catégories Matrimoniales et Relations de Proximité dans La Chine Ancienne*, which stimulated his interest in kinship. Fortuitously, he received an invitation to take advantage of a plan organized by the Rockefeller Foundation to host European intellectuals in the United States. Once safely ensconced in New York, Lévi-Strauss came into contact with the exiled surrealists André Breton and Max Ernst, as well as Franz Boas and Roman Jakobson, among others (Hénaff 1998, 251). His meeting and subsequent friendship with the latter proved to be decisive to Lévi-Strauss' development and he himself has described it as a "revelation" (Lévi-Strauss and Eribon 1991, 41). He worked occasionally at the Office of War Information (OWI) and taught courses at the New School for Social Research, at the New York Ecole Libre des Hautes Etudes and at Barnard College. After liberation, Lévi-Strauss returned to Paris and married Rose-Marie Ullmo. He returned to New York as cultural attaché where he remained until 1947 after which he again returned to Paris (Deliège 2004, 10).

Lévi-Strauss then published *Les Structures Elémentaires de la Parenté*

(*The Elementary Structures of Kinship*) (1949). In it he applied principles similar to those used by Jakobson in linguistics, to marriage rules. It was a work that provoked considerable controversy and debate both within and without the discipline of social anthropology, and it helped to establish Lévi-Strauss and the discipline in France. In 1950, with the aid of Georges Dumézil, Lévi-Strauss was elected to the fifth section of the Ecole Pratique des Hautes Etudes, the fifth section being devoted to the study of religions. His chair was in the comparative study of the religions of 'non-civilized' peoples that had previously been occupied by Léon Mariller, Marcel Mauss and Maurice Leenhardt (Hénaff 1998, 254). In 1954 Lévi-Strauss succeeded in changing its name to "Religions Comparées des Peuples Sans Ecriture" ("Comparative Religion of Peoples Without Writing"). He also published an introduction to a book about Marcel Mauss which, according to Johnson (2003, 69–70), constitutes an important introduction to Lévi-Strauss' shift in focus—after the publication of *The Elementary Structures of Kinship*—to modes of thought. In 1952 he published *Race et Histoire* ("Race and History"), a work commissioned by UNESCO (United Nations Educational, Scientific and Cultural Organization) which can be considered a political work and somewhat of a departure from the highly specialized and arcane *The Elementary Structures of Kinship*. In 1953 he was elected secretary-general of the International Council of Social Sciences. In 1954 he married Monique Roman. In 1955 he published *Tristes Tropiques*—again quite different in tone from his more narrowly anthropological or "scientific" writings and which Clifford Geertz would later describe as resembling, in its design and form, "the standard legend of the Heroic Quest" (Pace 1986, 21). Indeed, Lévi-Strauss would himself claim that, at the time of writing, he believed himself to be "committing a sin against science" (Lévi-Strauss and Eribon 1991, 58).

In 1958 Lévi-Strauss published *Anthropologie Structurale* (*Structural Anthropology*), a work that was to cement Lévi-Strauss' association with structuralism (Lévi-Strauss and Eribon 1991, 68). In 1959—and at the third attempt—he was elected to the Collège de France, taking the chair in social anthropology. In 1960 he gave his inaugural lecture and in the same year founded the Laboratoire d' Anthropologie Sociale and the year after, he helped set up the journal *L'Homme*. In 1962 two further books appeared—*Le Totémisme Aujourd'hui* (*Totemism*) and *La Pensée Sauvage* (*The Savage Mind*). Lévi-Strauss has described these texts as studies of "religious representations" and of the necessity, as he saw it, of freeing anthropology "from certain illusions that obscured the study of religion in preliterate societies" (Lévi-Strauss & Eribon 1991, 71). Moreover, the four volumes that began with *Mythologiques I: Le Cru et le Cruit*

(*The Raw and the Cooked: Introduction to a Science of Mythology*) in 1964 were completed in 1971 with the publication of *Mythologiques IV: L'Homme Nu* (*The Naked Man: Introduction to a Science of Mythology IV*). Certainly, the application of a structuralist approach to the study of so-called totemism, myth and *la pensée sauvage* constituted a radical departure from the received wisdom of the anthropological canon which until then had been defined by hierarchically organized binary pairs such as primitive : modern and religion : science, and established Lévi-Strauss as an eminently original—and demanding—thinker. Later, he would characterize that approach as a form of quixotism and as "an obsessive desire to find the past behind the present" (Lévi-Strauss and Eribon 1991, 94).

Given Lévi-Strauss' early sympathies with socialism and the writings of Proudhon and Marx, one might have expected him to have played some kind of a role in the events of 1968. However, Lévi-Strauss refused to give the uprising his blessing, and indeed condemned it in no uncertain terms (Lévi-Strauss and Eribon 1991, 80; Pace 1986, 189–90). In 1971 the essay "Race et Culture" ("Race and Culture") was published. It is widely seen as being complementary to the earlier "Race et Histoire" (Hénaff 1998, 256; Pace 1986, 192). In 1973 he was elected to the Académie Française

---

Biographical details at a glance:

- Claude Lévi-Strauss was born in 1908 in Brussels.
- In 1935 he left for Brazil to take a position at the new University of São Paulo.
- In 1940 he arrived in New York. He worked at the Office of War Information and taught courses at the New School for Social Research, at the New York Ecole Libre des Hautes Etudes and at Barnard College.
- In 1950 he was elected to the fifth section of the Ecole Pratique des Hautes Etudes, the fifth section being devoted to the study of religions.
- In 1953 he was elected secretary-general of the International Council of Social Sciences.
- In 1959 he was elected to the Collège de France, taking the chair in social anthropology.
- In 1960 he gave his inaugural lecture and in the same year founded the Laboratoire d' Anthropologie Sociale. In the same year he helped set up the journal *L'Homme*.
- In 1973 he was elected to the Académie Française.

---

and *Anthropologie Structurale Deux* (*Structural Anthropology II*) was published in the same year. 1978 saw the publication of *Myth and Meaning* the text of which came from the "Massey Lectures"—five radio broadcasts which he delivered in English for the Canadian Broadcasting Corporation (CBC) in December 1977 as part of a CBC series called "Ideas" (Lévi-Strauss 2001, vii; Hénaff 1998, 257). Lévi-Strauss retired in 1982 though he remained a member of the Laboratoire d' Anthropologie Sociale. *Le Regard Eloigné* (*The View from Afar*), a third collection of essays complementing the two volumes *Structural Anthropology*, was published in the following year. Although a number of other texts have appeared since then it is the texts indicated above that constitute the primary source materials for this book.

Synopsis of chapters

Chapter one focuses on Lévi-Strauss' methodological writings. Particular emphasis is placed on Lévi-Strauss' borrowings from linguistics and the works of Ferdinand de Saussure and Roman Jakobson, his formulation of social anthropology as the elucidation of unconscious, mental structures, and his repeated claim that his primary intellectual debt is to Rousseau. This chapter also references the importance of structuralism, and the so-called linguistic turn to social theory and philosophy more generally, in particular the influence of structuralism on anthropologists such as Rodney Needham and Edmund Leach—both of whom played pivotal roles in the introduction of Lévi-Strauss' writings to an English-speaking audience—Louis Dumont who applied structuralist principles to the analysis of hierarchy, caste and asceticism in India, on the anthropology of Southeast Asia and the influence of structuralism on the writings of Jacques Lacan, Louis Althusser, Michel Foucault and Jacques Derrida.

Chapter two concentrates on Lévi-Strauss' contribution to the study of kinship in which he, for the first time, proposed that social anthropology should be the study of cultural systems as systems of communication and exchange. Chapter three examines his intervention in the debate about so-called totemism. The chapter begins with an overview of the theories of Frazer and Malinowksi, Robertson Smith, Durkheim and Radcliffe-Brown and finally Freud in which so-called totemism was posed variously as the earliest form of social organization and as the earliest form of religion. Lévi-Strauss' dramatic reformulation of the question of totemism effectively marked its simultaneous dissolution as a discrete category of anthropological analysis. Chapter four examines the influential and voluminous writings on myth and explores Lévi-Strauss' claims that the function of myth is to mediate irreconcilable contradictions, that immanent within myth is the binary structure of the human mind and his linking of myth with language and music. Chapter five engages initially with the twin notions of *la pensée sauvage* and *bricolage* as a means of suggesting that Lévi-Strauss' anthropological writings form a whole devoted to the refutation of evolutionist thinking in social anthropology and the demonstration of two hypotheses: firstly that human beings have an innate capacity for the ordering and classification of their worlds—and that therefore there is no Archimedean point from which to declare one mode of ordering and classification superior to another—and secondly that the basis of culture lies in the biologically given structure of the human mind. The chapter then moves to consider two essays on shamanism in which Lévi-Strauss draws parallels between shamanism and psychoanalysis and in so doing departs from a strict structural analysis. We will also briefly consider his analysis of Caduveo art in which Lévi-Strauss' again seems to engage in a more normative socio-logical analysis where the focus is not so much on culture as ideology.

In chapter six the essay changes tack, away from Lévi-Strauss' narrowly anthropological or, as he himself might characterize them, "scientific" writings, to works that can be considered philosophical and political and indeed even as polemical. These include the essays "Race and History" and "Race and Culture," the final chapter of *The Savage Mind* in which Lévi-Strauss attacks the thinking of Sartre, and *Tristes Tropiques* in which Lévi-Strauss articulates a kind of "case for the defence" of non-literate societies against the violence and waste of 'the West', but also a defence of a rather ill-defined "Buddhism" and a hostile critique of an equally ill-defined "Islam." The final chapter will summarize the key theoretical, methodological and political issues raised from this critical reading of Lévi-Strauss' writings, seeking to situate these *vis-à-vis* contemporary debates in the study of religions, particularly with regard to recent methodological debates and disputes in the study of religions (Fitzgerald 2000; Flood 1999; Lawson and McCauley 1990; McCutcheon 1997; Penner 1989). As such, I will argue that Lévi-Strauss' work offers a critical point of departure through which to re-think the terms in which debates about theory and method in the study of religions have been conducted.

How to use this book

This book constitutes an introduction to Lévi-Strauss' writing taken as a whole, although the emphasis throughout is on his contribution to the study of religions. It is not therefore a substitute for Lévi-Strauss' writings, merely a guide. However, it should prove valuable to students and non-specialists alike, particularly those engaged in the study of myth (chapter four), shamanism (chapter five), religion as a mode of thought and the anthropology of religion (chapters three, four and five), structuralism and anthropology (chapters one and two), structuralism and so-called post-structuralism (chapter one), anthropology and politics (chapter six) and structuralism and the phenomenology of religion (chapters one and seven). Each chapter forms a self-contained whole including discussion of the relevant texts from Lévi-Strauss' *oeuvre* and appropriate critiques. As such, the chapters can be read singly, chronologically or otherwise.

Throughout the book I attempt to highlight the manner in which Lévi-Strauss asserts the scientificity of the structuralist approach in particular via his borrowings from structural linguistics and the writings of Saussure, Jakobson and Troubetzkoy without, however, losing sight of the other symbolic resources that he draws from, in particular Jean-Jacques Rousseau. Moreover, the critiques cited of the various aspects of Lévi-Strauss' thought—McKinnon's (2001) reading of his approach to kinship, Strenski's (1987) careful reading of Lévi-Strauss' work on myth and Derrida's (1997) critique of *Tristes Tropiques*—were selected precisely because they highlight the fact that Lévi-Strauss' structuralism very much reflects the concerns of Western philosophy and social theory—in other words, the questions it poses and the answers it generates are already theory-saturated. I would argue, then, that structuralism is far from the neutral, value-free or objective approach Lévi-Strauss says it is. As such, I have also attempted to show the limits of the structuralist approach, in particular its inability to reflexively question itself as a mode of producing knowledge and—with the emphasis placed by Lévi-Strauss on thought— the failure to account for the relation of modes of thought to social, political, economic and historically articulated structures and processes.

Chapter 1

Lévi-Strauss, linguistics and structuralism

The human sciences will be structuralist or they will not be at all...The ethnologist, faced with thousands of societies and the incredible multiplicity of facts, must do one of two things: Either he can only describe and take inventory of all this diversity, and his work will be very estimable but it will not be scientific. Or else he will have to admit that behind this diversity there lies something deeper, something common to all its aspects. This effort to reduce a multiplicity of expressions to one language, this is structuralism. Maybe someday it will no longer be called that; I don't know and I don't care. But the effort to find a deeper and truer reality behind the multiplicity of apparent realities, that seems to be the condition of survival for the human sciences, whatever the undertaking is called.

(Claude Lévi-Strauss, There are no Superior Societies)

According to Lévi-Strauss, the conjunction of structural linguistics and social anthropology is a "revolution" akin to a "paradigm shift," to borrow Kuhn's (1970) famous phrase, in the social sciences. "A transformation of this magnitude," he writes, "is not limited to a single discipline" (Lévi-Strauss 1993a, 33). As such, Lévi-Strauss confidently claims that structural linguistics will play a "renovating role with respect to the social sciences" (Lévi-Strauss 1993a, 33), an argument premised on the notion that structural linguistics is the only one of the social sciences "which can truly claim to be a science" (1993a, 31), and that social anthropology, at least until this momentous conjunction of forces, has lacked the necessary synthetic rigour through which it might properly call itself a science. The scope of this "revolution" becomes clear when Lévi-Strauss sketches the results or outcomes proceeding from the hoped for co-operation of linguists and anthropologists:

I should say that the most important results of such cooperation will not be for linguistics alone or for anthropology alone, or for both; they will mostly be for an anthropology conceived in a broader way—that is, a knowledge of man that incorporates all the different approaches which can be used and that will provide a clue to the way according to which our uninvited guest, the human mind, works (Lévi-Strauss 1993b, 79–80).

These claims and assertions that speak of a "transformation" not just in social anthropology but in the social sciences generally, suggest that Lévi-Strauss regarded "structuralism" as making possible, for the first time, a total science of humankind, indeed as offering a method that could be the skeleton key for the unlocking of the truth, ultimately, of the human mind. Post post-modernism, such a claim might feel antiquated or utopian at best, totalitarian at worst. Nevertheless, it is true to say that these kinds of pronouncements generated considerable effervescence across the human sciences, though Lévi-Strauss did himself urge caution and suggested that it was "absurd" to "assume that the structural method" was "aimed at acquiring an exhaustive knowledge of societies" (Lévi-Strauss 1993c, 82). Structuralism, then, became the subject of heated debate, controversy and criticism. If it promised anthropology and anthropologists an authority they had never previously enjoyed, the costs of such a scientificity were soon apparent: structuralism appeared to many to be arid, obscure and inhumane (Sturrock 1993, vii). Furthermore, it would be claimed by "the" structuralists themselves that structuralism and its offspring heralded the death of the author (Barthes 1977, 148), the death of the subject (Foucault 1992, 387; Lévi-Strauss 1966, 247) and the death of meaning, or at least (!) the death of meaning as the crystallized trace of authorial presence (Derrida 1997, 11). If that were not bewildering enough, the representationist theory of the sign and

---

In this chapter:

- Introduction to Lévi-Strauss' application of insights derived from structural linguistics to anthropology.

- Introduction to the ideas and critical terms developed by Ferdinand de Saussure and Roman Jakobson in their analyses of language including the idea of structure, diachrony/synchrony, *langue/parole*, signifier/signified, syntagm/paradigm and metonym/metaphor.

- Introduction to Lévi-Strauss' claim that immanent within symbol systems is the structuring activity of the mind.

- Introduction to Lévi-Strauss' borrowings from Jean-Jaques Rousseau.

- Introduction to the legacies of structuralism: Lévi-Strauss' influence on social anthropology and philosophy.

---

the symbol seemed destined to be abandoned in favour of a relational theory (Gellner 1986, 37) that would once and for all sever the assumed and longed for tie between words and things.

Whether or not you or I subscribe to the "anti-humanism" and the "anti-representationism" that are said to lie at the centre of structuralist thought, structuralism registered a significant turn to language in social theory (Callinicos 1999, 266) and this linguistic turn, at least that is, in its structuralist variant, assumed that everything—even cooking—was a language or, more prosaically, a code, to be deciphered. This had serious consequences for the ways in which language and subjectivity had conventionally been understood. As such, structuralist anthropology offered a completely new way of thinking about questions of culture and cultural difference.

Language had been seen as a transparent medium for expressing thoughts and for describing or re-presenting objects. In structuralist thought, however, language is understood quite differently. For structuralists, linguistic expressions—utterances or speech acts—are the products not of individual or authorial intentions, but are rather constituted in advance by a hidden or unconscious grammar. Furthermore, for structuralist anthropologists—or at least for Lévi-Strauss—cultures are thought of as analogous to languages and therefore as systems of relations constituted by "unconscious foundations" (Lévi-Strauss 1993d, 18). Cultural variation is understood as the differential permutation or transformation of a key binary opposition—that of nature to culture—that ultimately and finally points to the structure of the human mind. As such, culture is not so much the product of human action but a reflection of and a series of variations arising from the deep, binary structure that is held to be constitutive of the way human beings think. In other words, the mind is immanent in culture and therefore through the study of culture—of art works, myths, kinship systems, religious representations and so forth—the structure of the mind can be discerned. Through the study of culture—perhaps in particular the analysis of how nature is apprehended through culturally encoded categories and schemes of classification—inferences can be made about how human beings think (Leach 1974, 15).

In order to understand on what grounds Lévi-Strauss felt confident enough to give the conjunction of structural linguistics and social anthropology such importance, in this section of the essay it behoves us to set out however briefly the principal tenets of structural linguistics through the writings of two of its most well-known exponents, Ferdinand de Saussure and Roman Jakobson. Then we will be in a position to set out and assess the manner in which the study of language and the study of culture could be considered by Lévi-Strauss to be analogous enterprises. This will also allow us to do two things: first, to examine the way in which Lévi-Strauss has framed other sources and influences on his thinking and secondly, to consider the importance of structuralism as an intellectual movement and the extent of its influence both within and without social anthropology.

Structural linguistics

Ferdinand de Saussure was born in Geneva in 1857, and taught at the University of Geneva from 1891 until his death in 1913. The *Cours de Linguistique Générale* (*Course in General Linguistics*) was published in 1916 by two editors—Bally and Sechehaye who, incidentally, never attended Saussure's lectures—who collated and edited the notes taken by Saussure's students at the University of Geneva. The circumstances surrounding the publication of this text—a text central to structuralism—is somewhat ironic given that, effectively, the text has no author (Penner 1989, 134; Sturrock 1993, 4).

Saussure argued that language could be studied along two separate axes: the diachronic axis and the synchronic axis. A linguist studying language diachronically studies language as it changes through time. It was this method that characterized linguistics in the nineteenth century. The discovery that guided this course of enquiry was that different languages were related to one another. The task, then, was to establish relations between languages through comparison, and to elucidate the evolution or development of these languages from a presumed common ancestor (Jameson 1972, 5). By contrast, Saussure advocated the study of language along the synchronic axis. According to Saussure, although languages change—such as through contact with other languages—these changes rarely alter the fundamental way in which the language is constituted as a system. In other words, although change may occur at the level of words and utterances—at the level of *parole*—the grammar, centre or underlying *langue*, remains the same (Penner 1989, 138–140).

Saussure's division of the study of language into diachronic and synchronic approaches parallels his division of language itself into two elements, which he calls *langue* and *parole*. *Parole* refers to utterances or speech, and essentially denotes the surface of language. *Langue*, however, points to a powerful centre or underneath—a grammar that functions beyond conscious apprehension. Jameson (1972, 13) has suggested that the shift in the study of language that Saussure proposes—from diachrony to synchrony and from *parole* to *langue*—amounts to "a movement from a substantive way of thinking to a relational one" (1972, 13). As such, Saussure formulated the synchronic and diachronic approaches to the study of language in the following way:

> Synchronic linguistics will be concerned with logical and psychological connections between coexisting items constituting a system, as perceived by the same collective consciousness. Diachronic linguistics on the other hand will be concerned with connections between sequences of items not perceived by the same collective consciousness, which replace one another without themselves constituting a system. (Saussure in Sturrock 1993, 5)

Actually, Saussure never used the word "structure"—rather, he employed the term "system." Nevertheless, both terms imply a constellation of elements, for example a grammar that is stored in the "collective consciousness" of a putative language community. Though this grammar is not conventionally available for conscious recollection or elucidation, it governs or determines every act of speech and writing within that community and is as such complete at every moment (Jameson 1972, 6). Moreover, grammar, according to Saussure, is a social bond, which according to Jameson (1972, 27) is a notion not merely reminiscent of Durkheim's conception of the collective consciousness but one that was actually inspired by it:

> It is a fund accumulated by the members of the community through the practice of speech, a grammatical system existing potentially in every brain, or more exactly in the brains of a group of individuals; for the language is never complete in any single individual but exists perfectly only in the collectivity. (Saussure in Sturrock 1993, 9)

So far I have introduced two pairs of terms—diachronic and synchronic and *langue* and *parole*. The next pair of terms reflect Saussure's interest in words—what he calls signs—and these Saussure designates as the *signifiant* (signifier) and the *signifié* (signified) (Penner 1989, 136–37). Saussure is particularly interested in the relation of words to things, or the means by which, for example, the sound/word "horse" signifies or conjures up the concept of the four-legged beast we all know to be a horse. According to Saussure, a sign has two aspects: first there is the aspect of sound—the acoustic aspect—and secondly, there is the conceptual aspect, which, in this case, is the horse itself. These two aspects are mutually interdependent—"one can neither isolate sound from thought or thought from sound" (Saussure in Jameson 1972, 3). Saussure's central argument *vis-à-vis* the sign and its relation to a particular concept or object is that the sign is arbitrary and meaning therefore rests on social convention (Hawkes 1983, 25; Jameson 1972, 30; Sturrock 1993, 15). In other words, there is no reference or special relationship that ties the sign or word "horse" to the horse itself. Previous theorists of language assumed that language was basically a nomenclature, or a straight forward list or system for naming the things in the world. This kind of theory assumed that the world and its objects existed outside or before language and that language developed to enable the description or representation of "reality." For example, it could be argued that the conceptual aspect of the sign comes before its acoustic or graphic aspect, that meaning awaits expression or that the real, passive and supine, awaits accurate depiction. However, when signs are understood to refer internally to each other as elements of a language system rather than "outside" the system to objects in the world, we must contemplate an alternative relationship between words and objects. One consequence of the structuralist approach to language is then the suggestion that there is nothing outside or before language—rather, the world and its objects are disclosed to us through language (Sturrock 1993, 17).

If there is no direct relation between words and things, how is it that a word or sign is able to signify or carry meaning? According to Saussure, signification or meaning depends entirely on a sign's systematic or structural relations with other signs—relations that are conceived in terms of language as a system of differences:

> In the language itself, there are only differences. Even more important than that is the fact that although in general a difference presupposes positive terms between which the difference holds, in a language there are only differences, and no positive terms. Whether we take the signifier or the signified, the language includes neither ideas nor sounds existing prior to the linguistic system, but only conceptual and phonetic differences arising out of that system. In a sign, what matters more than any idea or sound associated with it is what other signs surround it. (Saussure in Sturrock 1993, 20)

According to Saussure, each element of the language system is "a form, not a substance" (Saussure in Sturrock 1993, 19). To appreciate this point one needs to understand Saussure's point concerning the dimensions of language: he argues that language functions along a horizontal or syntagmatic dimension, and a vertical, associative or paradigmatic dimension (Hawkes 1983, 26; Jameson 1972, 37; Penner 1989, 141; Sturrock 1993, 24). The meaning of a sign is, as such, generated through the conjunction of these two dimensions. *Vis-à-vis* the syntagmatic dimension, the meaning of a sign depends upon its juxtaposition with other signs in a sentence. Syntagmatic relations are, as such, relations of combination. *Vis-à-vis* the paradigmatic dimension, the meaning of a sign depends on words that are absent from a sentence, and, as such, paradigmatic relations are relations of substitution. To try to make this clear, I will set out an example. For instance, the sentence "horse my red is" has no meaning until its constituent words are placed or combined in the correct sequence along the horizontal or syntagmatic axis: "My horse is red." However, the meaning of this sentence is also dependent on certain, absent, associative or vertical or paradigmatic associations, which may be semantic or phonetic. Each word in the sentence connotes other words along the vertical or paradigmatic dimension. Phonetic associations for the word "horse" might include "hoarse," "coarse" or "hearse," while semantic associations might include the words "steed," "pony" or "mount." What is important to grasp here is that, according to Saussure, meaning has nothing to do with the speaking subject and her or his intentions, or any "natural" tie between a word and a thing. Words have no substantive value but are rather constituted negatively through the fact of their relationality with other words and to the system or structure taken as a whole. Meaning cannot be founded through reference to any ground outside language. Rather, meaning is produced through the mechanical interplay of the syntagmatic and paradigmatic dimensions of the language system. Structuralism, then, reveals a loss of authority in the speaking subject or language user, for it is the language system, centre or structure that organizes and generates meaning and not individual speakers.

Lévi-Strauss' work in anthropology would be profoundly influenced by the writings of Saussure. Like Saussure, he would focus not on superficial cultural variation but on an organizing grammar that lies beneath all cultural systems; like Saussure, his concern would not be with historical change but rather with the synchronic or timeless and systematic, constraining truth that lies behind cultural differences; he would regard the elements of culture such as kinship systems and local taxonomies or systems for the classification of plants and animals as self-referential systems much in the same way that Saussure considered language to be a system of relations; finally, Lévi-Strauss' approach to culture would be premised on the assumption that culture is structured like a language that if and when it has been correctly deciphered, would reveal a deep truth about the human mind and its workings.

Our attention to Jakobson will be confined to the distinction between the metaphoric and metonymic dimensions of language and the theory of distinctive features (Jakobson and Halle 1956). In a study of the language disorder aphasia, Jakobson claims that aphasia is constituted by two contrasting disorders: on the one hand, a disorder of "similarity" and on the other, a disorder of "contiguity" (Hawkes 1983, 76–77; Jakobson and Halle 1956, 55–82). Similarity, according to Jakobson, is associative and metaphoric and is connected with Saussure's vertical dimension of language, whereas contiguity is syntagmatic and thus metonymic and is as such parallel to Saussure's horizontal dimension of language (Jakobson and Halle 1956, 60):

> The combinative (or syntagmatic) process manifests itself in contiguity (one word being placed next to another) and its mode is *metonymic*. The selective (or associative) process manifests itself in similarity (one word or concept being 'like' another) and its mode is *metaphoric*. The 'opposition' of metaphor and metonymy therefore may be said to represent in effect the essence of the total opposition between the *synchronic* mode of language (its immediate, coexistent, 'vertical' relationships) and its *diachronic* mode, (its sequential, successive, linearly progressive relationships).
>
> (Hawkes 1983, 77–78)

Lévi-Strauss would distinguish between the paradigmatic/metaphoric and syntagmatic/metonymic dimensions or chains in his analyses of totemism, myth and *la pensée sauvage*. The metaphoric chain would refer to types of symbolization whereas the metonymic chain would point to specific symbols and their relation to a putative whole. Importantly, this has "pre-structuralist" precedents. First, in Freud's analysis of dreams

> the decisive question is whether the symbols and the temporal sequences used are based on contiguity (Freud's metonymic "displacement" and synecdochic "condensation") or on similarity (Freud's "identification and symbolism"). (Jakobson and Halle 1956, 81)

Secondly, in Frazer's analysis of magic in *The Golden Bough* the distinction drawn by Frazer between the "law of similarity" and the "law of contact" (Frazer 1991, 11) is, according to Leach (1974, 50–51), "practically identical to the Jakobson–Lévi-Strauss metaphoric-metonymic distinction" (see also Jakobson and Halle 1956, 81; Jameson 1972, 123).

Jakobson and Halle's theory of distinctive features is an attempt to generate a "minimum model" (1956, 40) that can explain the (universal) process through which children learn to master vowels and consonants as an integral step towards learning to utter meaningful sounds in a particular sequence as oppose to simply making noise. According to Jakobson and Halle, this process of discrimination begins with the child distinguishing between low frequencies and high frequencies or pitches which Jakobson and Halle represent in terms of a grave : acute opposition. Discrimination between pitches is accompanied by the ability to discriminate between higher and lower concentrations of energy or loudness, represented by Jakobson and Halle in terms of the opposition compact : diffuse. According to Jakobson and Halle, "no language lacks the oppositions grave/acute and compact/diffuse" (1956, 40) and they represent this basic structure— through which children acquire language—in terms of a triangle. Lévi-Strauss uses exactly the same model to create a "culinary triangle," which integrates the base opposition nature : culture with that of the opposition raw (unprocessed) : cooked (transformed). Therefore, whereas Jakobson and Halle's triangle represents the pair of oppositions grave : acute and compact : diffuse to portray the universal process through which children learn to distinguish vowels and consonants in the process of acquiring language, so Lévi-Strauss constructs "a culinary triangle to represent the binary oppositions normal/transformed and culture/nature, which are (by implication) internalized into the *eidos* of human culture everywhere" (Leach 1974, 26). *Vis-à-vis* the so-called culinary triangle, Lévi-Strauss notes that the use of fire for food preparation is a universal aspect of human behaviour, yet it is a remarkable behaviour because human beings do not actually have to cook their food in order to survive. According to Lévi-Strauss, human beings cook their food for symbolic purposes and thus cooking is a basic symbol through which human beings distinguish themselves from animals or nature (Leach 1970a, 129). For Lévi-Strauss, then, the process of discrimination central to the child's acquisition of language, where it learns to use meaningful sounds in specific sequences as opposed to merely making noise, is analogous to the process through which human beings "move," by cooking their food, from nature to culture.

Language and culture

Although we have intimated, in broad terms, the levels at which Lévi-Strauss drew on the insights of Saussure and Jakobson, some further explication is necessary as to how Lévi-Strauss could equate language with culture and claim that the study of each constituted parallel exercises. First, Lévi-Strauss borrows Troubetzkoy's four-step outline of the structural method:

> First, structural...[anthropology] shifts from the study of *conscious* ...[cultural] phenomena to the study of their *unconscious* infrastructure; second, it does not treat *terms* as independent entities, taking instead as its basis of analysis the *relations* between terms; third, it introduces the concept of *system*...finally, [it] aims at discovering *general laws*. (Lévi-Strauss 1993a, 33)

Secondly, in the essay "Linguistics and Anthropology,' Lévi-Strauss outlines three separate levels at which language and culture might confront one another. First, there is the relation between a language and a culture and the question as to what extent it is necessary to know a language in order to have some knowledge of a culture, as a mark of a particular population and territory where that language is spoken. Secondly, there is the relationship between culture and language or rather "the behaviour of culture as a whole toward language as a whole" (Lévi-Strauss 1993b,

68). Thirdly, there is the relation between linguistics (as a science) and social anthropology (as a science to be). It is this level which is, according to Lévi-Strauss, the most important. Lévi-Strauss remarks that "language can be said to be a *condition* of culture" (Lévi-Strauss 1993b, 68) because it is through language that one learns about one's own and other cultures and also because "the material out of which language is built is of the same type as the material out of which the whole culture is built: logical relations, oppositions, correlations, and the like" (Lévi-Strauss 1993b, 68–69).

It is precisely this latter assumption that, in his analysis of kinship, will allow Lévi-Strauss to suggest that kinship systems are like languages, such that "like phonemes, kinship terms are elements of meaning; like phonemes, they acquire meaning only if they are integrated into systems" (Lévi-Strauss 1993a, 34). In the structural analysis of kinship, then, Lévi-Strauss treats marriage rules and kinship systems as a form of communication wherein "the *women of the group*, who are *circulated* between clans, lineages, or families" are akin to "the *words of the group*, which are *circulated* between individuals", an analogy that allows Lévi-Strauss to claim "that the essential aspect of the phenomenon is identical in both cases" (Lévi-Strauss 1993e, 61). Assuming that this analogy between kinship systems and languages and women and words is both meaningful and productive, nevertheless, the question remains as to whether the analogy can be stretched further to encompass other aspects of social life such as art and religion (Lévi-Strauss 1993e, 62). However, Lévi-Strauss is not willing to ask this question except rhetorically, and the totality of his *oeuvre* indeed includes analyses of art and religion conducted precisely in structuralist terms. I will examine, in more detail, the specifics of Lévi-Strauss' approach to kinship and other aspects of culture and religion later in this book. For the time being it is sufficient to note in the first instance the influence and significance of structural linguistics on his thinking, secondly that for Lévi-Strauss, the study of language and the study of culture are analogous enterprises and thirdly that the structuralist approach is "the quest for the invariant, or for the invariant elements among superficial differences" (Lévi-Strauss 2001, 6).

Structure and structuralism

In *Tristes Tropiques*, Lévi-Strauss provides a number of clues as to his early intellectual inclinations. He claims to have rejected phenomenology and existentialism, the former for its privileging of experience, the latter because of its "over-indulgent attitude towards the illusions of subjectivity" (1992a, 58). Indeed, he appears to present a view reminiscent of Comte's in his posing of the relationship between philosophy and science:

> The raising of personal preoccupations to the dignity of philosophical problems is far too likely to lead to a sort of shop-girl metaphysics, which may be pardonable as a didactic method but is extremely dangerous if it allows people to play fast-and-loose with the mission incumbent on philosophy until science becomes strong enough to replace it: that is, to understand being in relationship to itself and not in relationship to myself. Instead of doing away with metaphysics, phenomenology and existentialism introduced two methods of providing it with alibis. (Lévi-Strauss 1992a, 58)

Lévi-Strauss' rejection of phenomenology and existentialism was, simultaneously a rejection of the dominant intellectual paradigms of the day. Instead, Lévi-Strauss identifies with Marx, Freud and geology, claiming that all three proceed in a similar manner in their common view that reality is not what it seems and that truth lies, as it were, hidden behind the real:

> At a different level of reality, Marxism seemed to me to proceed in the same manner as geology and psychoanalysis (taking the latter in the sense given by its founder). All three demonstrate that understanding consists in reducing one type of reality to another; that the true reality is never the most obvious; and that the nature of truth is already indicated by the care it takes to remain elusive. For all cases, the same problem arises, the problem of the relationship between feeling and reason, and the aim is the same: to achieve a kind of *superrationalism*, which will integrate the first with the second, without sacrificing any of its properties. (Lévi-Strauss 1992a, 57–58)

However, one should be wary of assuming that general statements such as these indicate anything more than the loosest sympathy, on Lévi-Strauss' part, with the writings of either Marx or Freud. Rather, Lévi-Strauss is noting an affinity between the approach taken by Marx and Freud to particular questions and problems, and his own approach to culture. For example, he argues that *Capital* "is a model constructed in the laboratory and set in motion by the author so he could view the results in conjunction with observed events" (Lévi-Strauss and Eribon 1991, 108), at once evading and disavowing the political project for which *Capital* was written, in favour of an exclusive focus on the manner or mode of production employed by Marx in his critique of capitalism. Moreover, these references to Marx, Freud and geology conceal certain critical differences in the concept of structure developed by Lévi-Strauss and that to be found in Marx' writings (Marx 1992, 424–28) or those of Freud (2003), differences altogether erased by Badcock who claims that "structuralism is in fact just a new version of psychoanalysis" (1975, 14).

According to both Merquior (1988, 8–9) and Gellner (1986, 136), anthropology before structuralism typically distinguished between structure and culture, with the latter assumed to be the epiphenomenal effect of the former. Indeed, for anthropology in its functionalist variant, structure referred to organization and patterned interaction. As Gellner memorably put it, "structure was…whom one could marry; culture was what the bride wore" (Gellner 1986, 136). In *structuralisme* (as Gellner would have it), it is culture that is privileged and is ascribed autonomy which perhaps makes Lévi-Strauss' initial focus on kinship somewhat incongruous (Gellner 1986, 137): indeed, Johnson (2003, 69) characterizes Lévi-Strauss' shift in emphasis from the analysis of kinship to totemism as a shift from "the study of the 'infrastructures' of social organization to the "superstructures" of religious representations." Nevertheless, in both functionalist and structuralist usages of the term, "structure" refers to patterns, repetitions and probabilities. According to Bauman (1999, 67), the promise of structuralism lies precisely in its attempt to offer a solution to the question of the relation between social structure and culture: whereas the former would relate to relations and constraints the latter would be the code "through which information…is expressed, conveyed, deciphered and processed." As such, we might understand Lévi-Strauss' anthropology as an inversion of that developed and pursued by Durkheim. If Durkheim's sociology proceeds "*from the mental to the social*" and from "belief to social structure" then Lévi-Strauss' moves "*from the social to the mental*" (Merquior 1988, 38), or from culture to a structuring pan-human mind.

What of this pan-human mind? Interestingly, Lévi-Strauss has described himself as "a hyper-Kantian" (Lévi-Strauss and Eribon 1991, 162), yet he makes almost no references in his anthropological writings to Kant (but see Lévi-Strauss 1992b, 10–11). Nevertheless, we can say that Lévi-Strauss' thought is Kantian to the extent that Lévi-Strauss accepts Kant's argument that things as they are cannot be known—rather, we can only know them through the biologically given apparatus of perception we call the mind. As Lévi-Strauss himself has said with regard to Kant, "the mind has its constraints, which it imposes on an ever-impenetrable reality, and it reaches this reality only through them" (Lévi-Strauss and Eribon 1991, 108). It is important to remember that when Lévi-Strauss refers to the unconscious it is precisely to this constitutive and structuring activity of the mind that he is pointing—"the unconscious activity of the mind consists in imposing forms upon content" (Lévi-Strauss 1993d, 21)—and not to any Freudian notion of (repressed) drives or instincts.

Lévi-Strauss' Kantianism, such as it is, is related to the guiding assumption that sits behind Lévi-Strauss' anthropological writings, namely that culture and cultural phenomena are like languages in that they are composed of a limited number of elements whose combination is regulated by laws or rules. Furthermore, cultures are essentially kaleidoscopic transforma-tions of a single organizing grammar (Lévi-Strauss 1966, 36), specifically the mind itself. However, if this is Kantianism, it is one without a transcen-dental subject (Ricoeur 2004, 33) or, alternatively as Hénaff contends, it is a "Leibnizianism without divine understanding" (Hénaff 1998, 109). Yet a Leibniz without God is surely an anti-Leibniz, and a Kant without a tran-scendental subject is similarly de-centred.

A view from afar?

Leaving arguments as to the philosophical underpinnings—or preten-sions—of Lévi-Strauss' writings to one side, and noting too that Lévi-Strauss has claimed that structuralism is not a philosophy (Lévi-Strauss 1981, 638), we must recognize the extent to which the language of the laboratory, of the experiment, of models and of model-building and the references to mathematics, physics, chemistry, cybernetics and so-called game theory in his writings suggest a style or mode of analysis and explanation based not in the face-to-face-ness of the field work encounter or even the classroom, but in the sterile calm and distance of the library reading room, and to be sure, some of Lévi-Strauss' comments appear to support this view. For instance, he has claimed that "*the anthropolo-gist is the astronomer of the social sciences*" (Lévi-Strauss 1993f, 378), and that "knowledge lies on the outside" (Lévi-Strauss and Eribon 1991, 154), both statements that imply the view that structuralist social science affords the investigator a privileged position in the study of social life that is simply not ordinarily accessible. Furthermore, in response to Norbert Wiener's critique of the social sciences and their alleged inherent lack of objectivity due to their implication in the very processes they seek to study, Lévi-Strauss claims that unconscious structures are not affected by obser-vation (Lévi-Strauss 1993e, 57; Merquior 1988, 66–67). Yet, at the end of *Totemism* Lévi-Strauss is critical of previous anthropological research on "primitive" classification and religious representations precisely because it did not "see" the phenomenon from within, being instead determined to "separate primitive institutions from our own" (1991, 103), while in the "Overture" to *The Raw and the Cooked* Lévi-Strauss speaks of "adopting the standpoint of a particular culture" (1992b, 1).

Lévi-Strauss, then, employs spatial metaphors to describe the structur-alist approach—metaphors both of distance and of proximity, of outside and of inside. But, the appeals to the rigour of science and objectivity and the entwined tropes of distance and the outside surely predominate. As such, we should also note that claims to scientific objectivity and authority in anthropology tend to be considered with some (justifiable) suspicion (Haraway 1991, 189) and have been challenged typically through recourse to arguments that stress the rhetorical or ideological nature of science as a discourse of distance, neutrality and so forth, or which alternatively emphasize the fact that anthropologists, like their informants or co-researchers, are thoroughly embedded in the world and that knowledge therefore arises not from a knowing subject measuring, weighing and assessing objects (facts) but rather through dialogue and encounter between co-subjects (Clifford 1986, 15; Gadamer 2004, 371; Habermas 2002, 295–96) in which facts can change under differing kinds of enquiry. However persuasive we may find these latter arguments—and they have their critics (Fardon 1990, 9–19; Gellner 1992, 25–26)—it is important to recognize that Lévi-Strauss is well aware of the fact that anthropological knowledge, like all other kinds, is mediated by the times and places in which we find ourselves:

> From the day we are born, our environment penetrates us through a thousand conscious or unconscious processes, with a complex system of references consisting in value judgements, motivations, and centres of interest (including the reflexive view of the historical development of our civilization imposed on us by our education)…we literally move along this system of references, and the exterior cultural realities can only be observed through the deformation imposed by it (when it does not go so far as to make it impossible for us to perceive any of it). (Lévi-Strauss 1994a, 340)

For Lévi-Strauss, then, knowledge is not purely a matter of disinterested observation from some monumental vantage-point. Rather, knowledge also arises out of historically situated contact, encounter and conversation. This is evident not only in his refutation of the evolutionist theory of history in "Race and History" (1994a) which I will return to later in this book, but also in his discussion of social anthropology and the training of anthropologists. In this discussion, field work emerges as a kind of alchemical *rite de passage* that inspires an "inner revolution that will make him [the anthropologist] into a new man" (Lévi-Strauss 1993f, 373). Here, disinterested observation is out, (gendered) *koinonia* in (Hénaff 1998, 24; Sontag 1970, 190–91).

Lévi-Strauss has, then, consistently privileged science and made use of science as a special discourse to give his own work authority, and as a means of legitimating an alliance of social anthropology with structural linguistics. Moreover, references to other thinkers such as Marx have tended to concentrate on the formal rather than the substantive aspects of their work. Lévi-Strauss' structuralism has tended to be represented by critics as a mode or style of analysis that is cold, dry and overly and overtly scientistic. However, as we have seen, Lévi-Strauss' views are somewhat more difficult to pin down. Things become even more complicated when we consider Lévi-Strauss' repeated tributes and references to Rousseau, a source of symbolic capital and prestige (if you will) quite different in kind to that generated by references to the likes of Roman Jakobson. Actually, Lévi-Strauss' engagements with the writings of Jean-Jacques Rousseau are part of a wider effort on Lévi-Strauss' part to develop on the one hand a very particular vision of social anthropology and its "mission" and, on the other, to articulate a humanism that does not take as its fundamental ground, the self-transparent individual, human subject. As such, Lévi-Strauss' assertion that "Rousseau did not restrict himself to anticipating ethnology: he founded it" (Lévi-Strauss 1994b, 35) depends on a conception of social anthropology as transformative not merely of the field worker him or herself as we saw above but of humankind as a whole, a transformation that has at its core a sense of "compassion" (Lévi-Strauss 1994b, 38) and which necessarily "places the other before the self" (Lévi-Strauss 1994b, 37) as a key element in what Lévi-Strauss calls "the technique of estrangement" (1994c, 272). The anthropologist is, for Lévi-Strauss, a stranger—an outsider—by profession.

Lévi-Strauss' references to Rousseau need to be understood as reflecting a second strand or current in his thought, of which we are beginning to see more evidence. This split is registered in the following reference in which Lévi-Strauss seems to equate his interest in Marx and Freud with reason, and his interest in Rousseau with passion: "Marx and Freud make me think. Rousseau sets me aflame" (Lévi-Strauss and Eribon 1991, 168). On the one hand, then, there is Lévi-Strauss the social scientist whose writings are highly specialized and narrow in their focus and, on the other, there is Lévi-Strauss the engaged public intellectual who is given to making rather more general and controversial statements. We will devote substantial space to Lévi-Strauss the political thinker towards the end of this book.

Structuralism and after

This chapter has been concerned with sketching some of the influences on Lévi-Strauss' thinking. Certainly we have not exhausted this line of enquiry: for example, no mention has been made so far of Mauss, though we shall have recourse to discuss Lévi-Strauss' debt to Mauss' *The Gift* (1954) in the following chapter. However, it is now necessary to briefly sketch the extent of Lévi-Strauss' and structuralism's influence both within and without the discipline of social anthropology.

Lévi-Strauss' writings caused quite a stir among British anthropologists. Rodney Needham and Edmund Leach, who were instrumental to the translation of Lévi-Strauss into English both critically engaged with his ideas (Leach 1974; Needham 1962 and 1971), and we will have reason to consider them in a little more detail in the following chapter. Louis Dumont's work on hierarchy in India (1980, 39) also introduced structural analysis to new areas of application (caste and asceticism) and a new audience. Moreover, between the 1950s and 1970s, structuralism was the theory of choice applied by European anthropologists to the study of Southeast Asian cultures and societies, though their American counterparts tended to apply the interpretive framework pioneered by Boas and taken further by Clifford Geertz in his work on Java. Indeed, structuralism's rise to eminence occurred at the very same time when the region as a region entered scholarly discourse (King and Wilder 2003, 313). Whereas American anthropologists directed their research towards interrogating processes of modernization and concomitant issues of national development and socio-cultural reproduction, European anthropologists, informed by Lévi-Strauss' structuralism, focused on Southeast Asia's minority cultures at the margins of the new states. Re-reading these ethnographies—many of which focused on religion, for example Endicott (1970) and Tambiah (1970)—one can only agree with King and Wilder's observation that, though "meticulous and thought provoking," they seem nevertheless rather "remote from the realities of political and economic development and change" (2003, 316). Unsurprisingly, structuralism no longer enjoys the prominence it once did in Southeast Asian studies, precisely because of its tendency to present cultures as systems seemingly cryogenically frozen in special chambers, untouched by the vicissitudes of time.

It was perhaps outside anthropology that structuralism was to have its greatest and most long-lasting impact. Jacques Lacan combined Saussurian linguistics and psychoanalysis while Louis Althusser attempted to transform Marx into a structuralist. Although he always repudiated the "structuralist," label, Michel Foucault's "archaeology" was a structuralist historiography, while Jacques Derrida's critiques of Saussure and Lévi-Strauss suggested not a post- or anti-structuralism but perhaps instead a revitalized and expanded one, inspired by Nietzsche. The success of these various enterprises—if judged by the amount of literature they have spawned—seems beyond question. Yet Lévi-Strauss has claimed that none of these thinkers are structuralists and indeed only the writings of Benveniste, Dumézil and himself warrant the label (Hénaff 1998, 4). Nevertheless, it would be churlish to ignore the influence of Lacan, Althusser, Foucault and Derrida on social theory and philosophy despite the apparent uncertainty of their relationship with structuralism even if we find ourselves disagreeing with almost everything they have to say. For example, Lacan's claim that "the unconscious is structured...like a language" (Lacan 1989, 234) is surely incoherent given that language is something acquired and as such belongs to the realm of culture whereas the unconscious, at least for Freud, was a realm of drives and instincts that constituted a threat to the "reality principle" precisely because it was not culture. If the principle of reality is threatened in Freud, Lacan's privileging of the signifier, where meaning or reference never arrives at a signified because each signifier slides inevitably into another, does away with reality altogether (Merquior 1988, 155): hence, the only "order" an individual can be born into is "symbolic."

According to Jameson, we can "understand the structuralist enterprise as a study of superstructures, or, in a more limited way, of ideology" (1972, 101; Lévi-Strauss 1966, 117). This may indeed offer a productive way to read Lévi-Strauss: whether it justifies a re-reading of Marx as an exemplar of structuralism is another matter. The structuralist insistence on the autonomy of the cultural rather than the epiphenomenal status of ideology and its determination by specific organizations of production and property in historical societies surely necessitates not the "demarcation" of a scientific Marx from some humanist imposter (Althusser 2005, 13), but rather his imaginative re-creation.

The "return" to Freud initiated by Lacan and the re-reading of Marx offered by Althusser via their engagements with Lévi-Strauss, Saussure and Jakobson are, to my mind, problematic. The writings of Michel Foucault at least display a reflexive awareness of the problems involved in the application of structuralist ideas to areas and questions they were not initially designed to address. Foucault's *The Order of Things: An Archaeology of the Human Sciences* (1992) is a detailed analysis of the "underlying rules, assumptions and ordering procedures" (Best and Kellner 1991, 41) that lie behind and regulate the distribution of statements in the Renaissance, Classical and Modern epochs. Rejecting any incremental or accumulative theory of knowledge, Foucault's emphasis is on discontinuity as one historically specific but also anonymous and indeed unconscious grammar or *episteme* is replaced by another, a move which allows Foucault to both reveal the birth of that "strange figure of knowledge called man" (1992, xxiv) and to envision its annihilation "like a face drawn in sand at the edge of the sea" (1992, 387). Stranger still, these *epistemes* float above the world, disconnected from institutions, states, economies and ways of life, as if discourses were autonomous and indeed constitutive of, reality (Hoy 1994, 4). Foucault's shift to so-called genealogy, according to Dreyfus and Rabinow (1983), implied the recognition on Foucault's part of the limitations of archaeology/structuralist historiography. Certainly, in *Discipline and Punish* (1979), Foucault explicitly sought to explicate the relations between discourses and particular institutions and institutional practices.

If Lacan, Althusser and Foucault attempted to combine certain insights from structuralism with other ideas and concerns, it could be argued that Derrida was simply taking the insights of Saussure to their logical conclusion. In particular, Saussure's idea of difference—through which he sought to demonstrate the lack of identity at the heart of the sign and that meaning was produced in the sign's relations with other signs rather than in its pointing to any thing outside the language system—is registered via the neologism "*différance*" to draw attention to this simultaneous differing and deferring and to the non-referentiality of the sign.

Différance is central to the idea of "deconstruction" (Derrida 1997, 24 and 158) which, according to Derrida, is not a method or formal procedure, but rather an attitude or stance that seeks not to dis-assemble texts with tools smuggled in from the outside, but is rather a mode or manner of revealing or witnessing the way in which texts undo or deconstruct themselves because, according to Derrida, language and meaning are always beyond the conscious control of any given author. As such in *Memoires for Paul de Man* Derrida writes that

> there is always already deconstruction, at work in works, especially in literary works. Deconstruction cannot be applied, after the fact and from the outside, as a technical instrument of modernity. Texts deconstruct *themselves* by themselves. (Derrida in Moran 2000, 452)

Derrida's insight is that texts weave the illusion of possessing a central meaning and he claims that a deconstructive reading reveals that such a core meaning is never in fact attained and indeed is subverted by other meanings within the text, a point demonstrated quite brilliantly in the essay "Plato's Pharmacy" (Derrida 2004).

Perhaps deconstruction offers a kind of liberation from the weight of crystallized interpretations embedded in the tomes of the academy—a means, also perhaps of demonstrating the limits of reason and of philosophy as a sedimented tradition of interpretation. In the essay "Structure, Sign and Play in the Discourse of the Human Sciences" (2002) Derrida suggests that the turn to language constitutes a rupture with what we might call the philosophy of the centre:

> The entire history of the concept of structure...must be thought of as a series of substitutions of centre for centre...[and] the history of metaphys-

ics…is the history of these metaphors and metonymies…It could be shown that all the names related to fundamentals, to principles, or to the centre have always designated an invariable presence—*eidos, archē, telos, ousia* (essence, existence, substance, subject) *alētheia*, transcendentality, consciousness, God, man, and so forth. (Derrida 2002, 353)

Precedents for this rupture are to be found, according to Derrida, in the writings of Nietzsche, Freud and Heidegger (2002, 354) and indeed in ethnology (2002, 356). Lévi-Strauss' own work—particularly his analyses of myth where myths refer only to other myths (2002, 361–65) and in *Tristes Tropiques* where Derrida identifies "a sort of ethic of presence, an ethic of nostalgia for origins, an ethic of archaic and natural innocence, of a purity of presence and self-presence in speech" (2002, 369)—is read by Derrida as embracing both a nostalgia for origins and a "Nietzschean *affirmation*, that is the joyous affirmation of the play of the world" (2002, 369). These "two interpretations of interpretation" (2002, 370) are irreconcilable and yet share a common ground. It is not, says Derrida, a matter of choosing between them—nostalgia (for presence) or affirmation (of indeterminacy or absence)—rather, it is in the tension of the in-between that "there is a kind of question…we are only catching a glimpse of today" (2002, 369). Lévi-Strauss, then, to his liking or not, is positioned by Derrida as a harbinger of a post-modern incredulity for origins, foundations and the self-present and transparent certainty of reason and of "man."

Summary

In this chapter I have sketched on the one hand some of the main influences on Lévi-Strauss' thinking and, on the other, the influence of structuralism on anthropology and social theory and philosophy more generally. In what follows we will engage more closely with Lévi-Strauss' writings, keeping sight at all times of structuralism as the product of particular circumstances in the history of Western thought, despite Lévi-Strauss' insistence that we look the other way.

Chapter 2

Kinship as communication

> If the incest prohibition and exogamy have an essentially positive function,
> if the reason for their existence is to establish a tie between men which the
> latter cannot do without if they are to raise themselves from a biological to
> a social organization, it must be recognized that linguists and sociologists
> do not merely apply the same methods but are studying the same thing.
> Indeed, from this point of view, "exogamy and language...have fundamen-
> tally the same function—communication and integration with others."
>
> (Claude Lévi-Strauss, *The Elementary Structures of Kinship*)

The Elementary Structures of Kinship (1969) is one of those works that
appears to come outside the corpus of texts that would conventionally
fall under a study of religions gaze. Given that studies of kinship seem to
belong to anthropology's past, beyond a narrow community of specialists
it probably also falls beyond the attention of most students of anthropology as well. This is regrettable given that it is here that Lévi-Strauss first
attempts to apply the insights obtained from structural linguistics to social
anthropology. In this chapter we will first outline the basic argument of

---

In this chapter:

- Introduction to *The Elementary Structures of Kinship*.
- Lévi-Strauss' application of ideas derived from structural
  linguistics to the problem of incest and exogamy.
- Lévi-Strauss' re-formulation via Mauss of kinship networks
  as exchange and communication systems.
- Lévi-Strauss' opposition of nature and violence to culture
  and exchange.
- Critiques of Lévi-Strauss' approach to kinship: Edmund
  Leach, Rodney Needham, Pierre Clastres and Susan
  McKinnon.

---

the work supplemented by references to essays published in *Structural Anthropology* volumes I and II and *The View from Afar* focusing in particular on Lévi-Strauss' claim that kinship is a form of exchange that produces solidarity between groups and constitutes the moment of passage from nature to culture and from violence to civility. Secondly, we will examine a number of critiques including those of Leach (1974), Needham (1962 and 1971), Clastres (1994a) and McKinnon (2001).

Lévi-Strauss' analysis of kinship is an analysis of rules—rules which are largely unconscious but which nevertheless govern behaviour in law-like fashion. In the preface to the first edition of *The Elementary Structures of Kinship*, Lévi-Strauss distinguishes between "elementary structures of kinship" and "complex structures," the first (apparently) equivalent to so-called preferential marriage where there is "almost automatic determination of the preferred spouse" and second to contemporary societies where other "economic or psychological" mechanisms come into play in the choice of marriage partner (1969, xxiii). These claims are then qualified— "the strictest elementary structure retains a certain freedom of choice, while even in the vaguest complex structures this choice is subject to certain limitations" (1969, xxiv). It is then claimed that the work constitutes an "introduction to a general theory of kinship systems" (1969, xxiv) which is followed by the conventional caveats *vis-à-vis* the possibility of errors in fact and in interpretation. However, a different tone is sounded in the final sentences of the preface where physics and sociology are sutured together via the claim that both study "organization." Once again, then, we find Lévi-Strauss hinting that the time has come for sociology (social anthropology) to claim the status of a "science." Indeed in chapter XIV, the appendix to part one of *The Elementary Structures of Kinship* which was composed by André Weil at Lévi-Strauss' behest, we find an attempt to demonstrate how Murngin "marriage laws can be interpreted algebraically" (1969, 221). This must surely be read as an attempt to give the anthropological analysis of kinship in particular and anthropological analyses of culture in general greater explanatory power by trying to demonstrate that cultures can be broken down and explained using mathematical models, a strategy that is repeated in Lévi-Strauss' work on myth (Lévi-Strauss 1993g, 228).

In the preface to the second edition some qualifications to the statements and claims made in the preface to the first edition are offered in light of criticisms by Rodney Needham. However, Lévi-Strauss also criticizes Needham, the translator of the English edition, for misunderstanding his argument, in particular his apparent claim that the so-called elementary structures are equivalent to so-called preferential marriage. As such, Lévi-

Strauss states that "an elementary structure can be equally preferential or prescriptive" (1969, xxxiii), which has more than a hint of him wanting not just to eat his cake but indeed to take possession of the entire bakery. Amusingly, these arcane disputes are further alluded to in the editor's note, where unusual effort is expended in demonstrating the rigour of the translation, and complaints are made against Lévi-Strauss who apparently abstained from examining the translated manuscript before it went to press. With the privilege of hindsight, such disputes surely appear petty, but the viciousness with which they were pursued is no doubt a function of the fact that so little was at stake.

Incest and exogamy

As we saw in the previous chapter, central to Lévi-Strauss' structuralism is the transformative opposition, nature : culture. In the opening two chapters of *The Elementary Structures of Kinship*, Lévi-Strauss engages in discussion of the problem of incest because it is "at once social, in that it is a rule, and pre-social in its universality" (1969, 12). In other words, the incest prohibition provides fertile ground for introducing structural analysis to social anthropology precisely because it appears to be a point of transition between nature and culture. Indeed, in terms that echo Freud, Lévi-Strauss states that the prohibition against incest "is at once on the threshold of culture, in culture, and in one sense…culture itself" (1969, 12).

Lévi-Strauss moves on to examine a number of anthropological theories that have been proffered to explain the incest prohibition: the biologism of Maine and Morgan, the pyschologism of Ellis and Westermack, and the social explanation of Durkheim which was based on the now discredited theory of the universality of so-called totemism (see chapter three) are all discussed and dismissed. Lévi-Strauss then states, once again in terms reminiscent of Freud in *Totem and Taboo*, that the incest prohibition "is the fundamental step…by which…the transition from nature to culture is accomplished" (1969, 24) and a little later, that it is a rule which, taken negatively, prevents the person from doing exactly as he or she pleases and which taken positively initiates organization, specifically via exogamous marriage (1969, 43). As such, the prohibition against incest is transformed, by the steady hand of Lévi-Strauss, into "a rule of reciprocity" and he further claims that the prohibition "is instituted only in order to guarantee and establish, directly or indirectly, immediately or mediately, an exchange" (1969, 51).

Kinship as communication

The incest prohibition, then, initiates exogamous exchange between human groups because daughters must be given away and wives acquired from strangers. Lévi-Strauss calls this the "principle of reciprocity" and he cites Mauss' seminal work *The Gift* (1954)—which incidentally should probably be read as a critique of the cold instrumentalism of *homo economicus* and capitalism—in which Mauss demonstrated that in so-called primitive societies exchange is not engaged in purely for economic advantage: first, the commodities exchanged have more than mere monetary value while second, the obligation on the part of the receiver to give in turn, establishes a relation that is but one element in a total system of transactions that establish, in Mauss' words, "civility" (1954, 81) between and among groups such that mutual reciprocity comes to replaces violence. The "tense experience" (Lévi-Strauss 1969, 60) that is the meeting of strangers—a meeting that could quite possibly be an occasion for fighting—is thus mollified through the exchange of gifts.

According to Lévi-Strauss, "exchange, as a total phenomenon, is from the first a total exchange, comprising food, manufactured objects, and that most precious category of goods, women" (1969, 60–61). Importantly, the exchange of women is conceived by Lévi-Strauss as the motor of exchange generally, with exchange conceived as the prerequisite for solidarity between human groups. Thus,

> a continuous transition exists from war to exchange, and from exchange to intermarriage, and the exchange of brides is merely the conclusion to an uninterrupted process of reciprocal gifts, which effects the transition from hostility to alliance, from anxiety to confidence, and from fear to friendship.
> (1969, 67–68)

Exogamy as the exchange of women, then, constitutes a form of communication between human groups, and this is made explicit in the essay "Language and the Analysis of Social Laws" in which Lévi-Strauss claims that "the *women of the group*, who are *circulated* between clans, lineages, or families" are akin to "the *words of the group*, which are *circulated* between individuals," an analogy that allows Lévi-Strauss to claim "that the essential aspect of the phenomenon is identical in both cases" (1993e, 61). However, as Merquior points out, "Levi-Strauss cannot resist...adding a typical masculine quip: yet unlike women, he says, words do not talk..." (1988, 45). (We will have reason to question Lévi-Strauss' rendering of women as goods and as words spoken by men later in this chapter). In the concluding chapter of the work, Lévi-Strauss informs us that the institution of exogamy means that "the biological family can no longer stand apart, and the bond of alliance with another family ensures the dominance of the social over the biological, and of the cultural over the natural" (1969, 479), and that the prohibition against incest as a rule "obliging the mother, sister or daughter to be given to others" is "the supreme rule of the gift" (1969, 481).

The question of the incest prohibition, exogamy, marriage and kinship is "solved" once and for all, then, by a structural mode of analysis based not in detailed fieldwork observation but rather through a close reading of the anthropological canon: historical analysis is similarly eschewed in favour of an approach that focuses upon the relations between entities and that assumes, in the study of social life that—as Lévi-Strauss' approving quotation from E.B. Tylor's *Primitive Culture* at the beginning of the work spells out—"if law is anywhere, it is everywhere" (1903, 24) (but see Lévi-Strauss' essay "Cross-Readings" 1985a). Lévi-Strauss may well have been writing against an evolutionist anthropology that had assumed monogamy to be the preserve of allegedly civilized peoples (Lévi-Strauss 1985b, 39). But just as the evolutionists had sought to discover the origins of culture in historical laws of development so Lévi-Strauss seeks the same in a law of the human mind. For example, in his analysis of so-called dual organization, Lévi-Strauss states that in order to "understand their common basis, enquiry must be directed to certain fundamental structures of the human mind, rather than to some privileged region of the world or to a certain period in the history of civilization" (1969, 75). Elsewhere, we find Lévi-Strauss re-stating his conviction that beneath the apparent diversity and even tumult of facts (kinship practices) there is, nevertheless, order. As such,

> rules that seem to be the most contradictory actually illustrate various modalities of exchange of women between human groups…following long or short cycles of reciprocity, which can be determined despite the apparent diversity of beliefs and customs.
>
> (Lévi-Strauss 1985c, 35–36)

Critiques of Lévi-Strauss' approach to kinship:

- Edmund Leach argues that specific kinship terms must be understood in terms of their socio-cultural context.
- Rodney Needham argues that Lévi-Strauss has ignored evidence in the interests of constructing a grand theory.
- Pierre Clastres and Susan McKinnon demonstrate that the key terms of Lévi-Strauss' argument are prefigured in European ideas about civility, paternity and gender.

The British critique

Edmund Leach's engagement with Lévi-Strauss is at once critical and constructive: indeed, Leach has written a number of essays about Lévi-Strauss, particularly about his approach to myth but also *vis-à-vis The Elementary Structures of Kinship*. In the study of kinship, writes Leach, anthropologists have paid particular attention to the terms used in different cultures to refer to or indeed produce relatedness between individuals. Whereas British anthropologists have tended to argue that different types of "kin term system are a response to different patterns of social organization" (1974, 106), Lévi-Strauss maintains that systems of kin terms are combinations or syntagmatic expressions of a single underlying grammar. The upshot of this is that Leach charges Lévi-Strauss with ignoring certain facts in favour of constructing a grand theory. Indeed, Leach claims that Lévi-Strauss' work on kinship is actually the least important (1974, 4) —because to his mind it is the least successful—part of Lévi-Strauss' considerable *oeuvre*.

Rodney Needham's engagement with Lévi-Strauss can only be described as schizophrenic. In *Structure and Sentiment: A Test Case in Social Anthropology* (1962), Needham engages in a passionate defence of *The Elementary Structures of Kinship*: for example, at this stage he notes the apparent confusion in Lévi-Strauss' equation of "preferential marriage" with "elementary structures" where the first category implies a choice in the selection of a spouse and the latter category implies not choice but prescription (1962, 8–12) yet he charitably represents this terminological confusion as a pseudo-problem only. As such, Needham feels able to conclude the work by claiming that "Lévi-Strauss' argument [in *The Elementary Structures of Kinship*] is not only essentially correct, but uniquely enlightening in its consequences" (1962, 126).

However, in his introduction to *Rethinking Kinship and Marriage*—published two years after *The Elementary Structures of Kinship* where Lévi-Strauss memorably accused Needham of a "fundamental misunderstanding" (1969, xxxiii) of his work —Needham takes a quite different tack. Now Lévi-Strauss is a target, and the pot shots and strafing come thick and fast. Now *The Elementary Structures of Kinship* is "idiosyncratic and baffling" such that it may even "defy a coherent interpretation" (1971, xciii). Needham claims that mistakes and contradictions can be found on almost every page, and that "it is an arguable matter whether there is a single theoretical proposition in it which is both novel and valid" (1971, xciv).

Of course, it's not all insults. Beneath the vitriol there is an argument— if, that is, one can be bothered to find it—and it rests in the first instance on that rather tiring Anglo-Saxon distrust of grand theory and the alleged French disdain for the facts. Thus we are told that "empirical demonstration must alone decide the issue" (1971, xcv), as if facts are facts whatever the lens used to see them or the framework applied to interpret them. Secondly, Needham turns to nominalism to argue that there is no such "thing" as "kinship:"

> I am not denying, therefore, that the word 'kinship' is useful; and still less should I wish to try to reform our professional vocabulary by narrowing the definition of the word, or, on the other hand, by urging that it be abandoned altogether. What I am saying is that it does not denote a discriminable class of phenomena or a distinct type of theory…anthropologists do often get into trouble, of a time wasting and discouraging sort, when they argue about what kinship really is or when they try to propound some general theory based on the presumption that kinship has a distinct and concrete identity. To put it very bluntly, then, there is no such thing as kinship and it follows that there can be no such thing as kinship theory. (Needham 1971, 5)

Lévi-Strauss is found guilty then, of that most heinous of crimes—"of trying prematurely to construct a grand theory" (1971, xcv)—impelling this reader at least to imagine Needham thinking of ways to get even with his dastardly snail-eating adversary, the pair of them proving surely beyond doubt that their trade in insults demands we recognize that war is not the absence of exchange or reciprocity but rather its continuation by other means.

Reciprocity and the problem of war

We have already noted the extent to which Lévi-Strauss' analysis of kinship depends on a very specific conception of culture and solidarity, namely that exogamy or the exchange of women constitutes the moment of transition from nature to culture and that this moment is, simultaneously, the point of transition from war to peace or from violence to civility. As such, Pierre Clastres argues that where "violence is dealt with [in the ethnography of 'primitive' societies]…it is primarily to show how these societies work toward controlling it, codifying it, ritualizing it, in short, tend to reduce if not abolish it" (1994a, 139). Indeed, Lévi-Strauss considers the question of war in only one essay ("Guerre et Commerce Chez les Indiens de l'Amérique du Sud" ["War and Commerce Among the Indians of South America"], 1943) where he argues that war and commerce cannot be considered in isolation and indeed constitute "a single and identical social process" such that "commercial exchanges represent potential wars peacefully resolved, and wars are the outcome of unfortunate transactions" (Lévi-Strauss in Clastres 1994a, 149–50), a position that is repeated again in *The Elementary Structures of Kinship* (1969, 67–68).

According to Clastres, Lévi-Strauss adopts a position that is both inverse and symmetrical to that taken by Hobbes in his simultaneously liberal and illiberal (Held 1985, 5) analysis of human nature and the state. Hobbes had argued that human life in the state of nature is "solitary, poor, nasty, brutish and short" (Hobbes 1985, 69) due to the fundamentally egotistical and aggressive character of human nature, a fact that, according to Hobbes, necessitates the creation of a strong state to watch over society in order that the baser human instincts can be subject to regulation and control. According to Hobbes, it is then in the "contract" entered into by a people and a state that the transition to civility is accomplished. Lévi-Strauss, by contrast, makes exogamy and the exchange of women and the increasing integration of human groups thereby engendered first in the symmetrical exchange engaged in between two exogamous groups, secondly in the symmetrical but delayed exchange found in patri-lateral cross-cousin marriage and thirdly in the delayed asymmetrical exchange found in matri-lateral cross-cousin marriage, the primary means by which human groups communicate with each other and ultimately overcome the urge to violence. Thus, for Lévi-Strauss, exchange/culture is positive, and war/nature—as the absence of exchange and therefore of communication—is negative, whereas for Hobbes the state—as the overcoming of violence—is positive while the state of nature, which is the condition of all against all, is given negative value.

If Lévi-Strauss equates war and violence with a pre-cultural condition, Clastres argues that war is a cultural activity that belongs "to the being of primitive society" (1994a, 152). Further, where for Lévi-Strauss war and violence exist on a continuum at whose opposite pole lies the realm of culture and exchange, for Clastres war is the realization of a "sociological will" (1994a, 153) in which so-called primitive societies assert their autonomy and independence in order to preserve an ideal state of autarchy (1994a, 154). Just as Lévi-Strauss himself has argued that so-called primitive societies are "cold" and are societies-against-entropy or societies-against-history such that primitivity is a "choice" they have made (Lévi-Strauss 1994d, 28), so Clastres argues that war, as a logic of dispersion and atomization, amounts to a state of being that has been "chosen" as an alternative to life permanently crystallized by the centripetal logic of a state:

> What is the function of primitive war? To assure the permanence of the dispersion, the parcelling, the atomization of the groups. Primitive war is the work of a *centrifugal logic*, a logic of separation, which is expressed from

time to time in armed conflict. War serves to maintain each community's political independence. As long as there is war, there is autonomy: this is why war cannot cease, why it must not cease, why it is permanent. War is the privileged mode of existence of primitive society, made up of equal, free and independent socio-political units: if enemies did not exist, they would have to be invented...What is primitive society? It is a multiplicity of undivided communities which all obey the same centrifugal logic. What institution at once expresses and guarantees the permanence of this logic? It is war, as the truth of relations between communities, as the principal sociological means of promoting the centrifugal force of dispersion against the centripetal force of unification. The war machine is the motor of the social machine; the primitive social being relies entirely on war, primitive society cannot survive without war. The more war there is, the less unification there is, and the best enemy of the State is war. Primitive society is against the State in that it is society-for-war. (Clastres 1994a, 164–166)

It appears, to this reader at least, that Clastres' intervention demonstrates the extent to which Lévi-Strauss' analysis reflects and is embedded within a European philosophical train of thinking that begins with Hobbes and which therefore impels us to raise questions about Lévi-Strauss' claims to the objectivity and scientificity of his analysis of kinship. Lévi-Strauss claims that the "elementary structures" his analysis uncovers are located at the unconscious level of culture, and because these structures are unconscious they are immune from contamination by any potential observer. Clastres' surely problematic ontological claims about savages and primitives aside, Lévi-Strauss' assumptions about nature and culture and violence and civility—assumptions which structure his analysis of kinship—may well not be empirically founded but might just as well be understood as being rooted in a tradition of thought peculiar to the very "corner" of the globe in which Lévi-Strauss has lived and worked for the majority of his life.

The paternity of culture

McKinnon's (2001) detailed and intelligent critique of Lévi-Strauss' *The Elementary Structures of Kinship* is worth recapitulating whole, as it reveals not merely the gender-blindness that seems to pervade pretty much Lévi-Strauss' entire corpus of writings, but also the extent to which the supposed scientificity afforded to anthropology by an alliance with linguistics is a mirage and that indeed Lévi-Strauss' analysis of kinship is deeply intertwined with culturally and historically specific values and ideas about paternity.

McKinnon begins her essay by stating her interest in "the association between paternity, kinship, economy, and the evolutionary forces that are thought to bring about culture in...social scientific origin stories" (2001, 277). She then claims that in *The Elementary Structures of Kinship*, Lévi-Strauss' "narrative moves from the initial isolation of natural, bounded consanguineal [consanguinity means sharing descent from a common ancestor with another person] groups through an all-or-nothing transformation to establish relations of reciprocity, and then increasing states of inclusiveness and integration" (2001, 278). Lévi-Strauss' story (note McKinnon's terminology) begins, then, with the family, and it seeks to work out how structured sociality could emerge from such a biological unit:

> As Edward Burnett Tylor understood a century ago, the ultimate explanation is probably found in the fact that man knew very early that he had to choose between "either marrying-out or being killed-out:" the best, but not the only, way for biological families not to be driven to reciprocal extermination is to link themselves by ties of blood. Biological families that wished to live in isolation, side by side with one another, would each form a closed group, self-perpetuating and inevitably prey to ignorance, fear, and hatred. In opposing the separatist tendency of consanguinity, the incest prohibition succeeded in weaving the web of affinity that sustains societies and without which none could survive. (Lévi-Strauss 1985b, 54–55)

Whereas for evolutionist anthropologists such as Morgan the family was the product of a long process of civilization from an originary primitive condition marked by promiscuity and a lack of differentiation, for Lévi-Strauss the family unit is there right from the beginning—it is eminently natural. The work of culture, then, lies in relating pre-given categories or units into a generalized order of sociality (2001, 290).

Furthermore, McKinnon notes that this generalized sociality is not only dependent on reciprocal exchange but also on the rationing of scarce produce (Lévi-Strauss 1969, 32). Lévi-Strauss argues that women are scarce because men are inherently polygamous and women are in-equally desirable (Lévi-Strauss 1969, 37–38) (his inability to imagine a situation of polyandrous women and in-equally desirable men is surely telling). As McKinnon notes, "in a remarkable combination of appeals to biology, innate tendencies, and historical reconstruction, Lévi-Strauss fabricates "the system of the scarce woman" in order to motivate the institution of the incest taboo" (McKinnon 2001, 292). The incest taboo then serves to authorize equal competition—a free-market, if you will—between men, and the equitable distribution and consumption of women for and by men. Thus, what changes in the transition from nature to culture is that "the system shifts from one of unregulated consumption ("keeping to oneself") with its hierarchical implications to one of regulated market exchange with its egalitarian consequences (for men, but not for women)" (2001, 294). In other words, Lévi-Strauss' story begins with the release or expulsion of daughters from the incestuous confines of the family and ends with innate tendencies to excessive accumulation and consumption (polygamy) regulated and controlled by the incest rule and exogamy as the circulation of women-as-scarce-commodity. A liberal model of capitalist exchange thus wins out over the model of the planned, self-sufficient economy, as might be deduced from Lévi-Strauss' references to credits, cycles, speculation, securities and profits (Lévi-Strauss 1969, 265–66). Ironically, however, *The Elementary Structures of Kinship* ends with a reference to an Andaman myth of the life to come which allegedly describes "the bliss of the hereafter as a heaven where women will no longer be exchanged, i.e., removing to an equally unattainable past or future joys, eternally denied to social man, of a world in which one might *keep to oneself*" (1969, 497). McKinnon pointedly adds the missing word from this strange refrain—"in which one might *keep women to oneself*" (2001, 297).

Summary

In this chapter we have considered Lévi-Strauss' analysis of kinship—the first time he applied the methods and assumptions of structural linguistics to a problem in social anthropology. In his analysis of kinship we can see the essentials of Lévi-Strauss' approach in operation: a mass of conflicting data is reduced to an invariant rule or general law—chaos is transformed into order (chapter by chapter, I will demonstrate that this also characterizes Lévi-Strauss' approach to totemism and myth). Yet, given Lévi-Strauss' emphasis on the integrative consequences of the incest prohibition and exogamy/reciprocal exchange, we might ask to what extent is the analysis structuralist or, for that matter, functionalist? (Lawson and McCauley 1990, 42). Moreover, is this approach to kinship "objective" as Lévi-Strauss would have us believe, or does it merely re-articulate the tropes, concerns and prejudices of white, Western liberalism?

Chapter 3

The illusion of totemism

Natural species are chosen not because they are "good to eat" but because they are "good to think." (Claude Lévi-Strauss, *Totemism*)

Implicated from the very beginning in early anthropological thinking about on the one hand incest, exogamy and the origins of society and on the other, fetishism, magic and the origins of religion, was the category "totemism." In this chapter we will begin by tracing the formation of the category through the writings of Frazer and Malinowski, Robertson Smith, Durkheim and Radcliffe-Brown and Freud. This survey, for the sake of brevity, will not be exhaustive. These thinkers were chosen because of the importance of their contributions not merely to the analysis of totemism but to the anthropology of religion generally, and it should be noted that these scholars do not neatly correspond to those discussed by Lévi-Strauss in either *Totemism* or *The Savage Mind*. Nevertheless, draw-

---

In this chapter:

- Introduction to *Totemism*.
- Introduction to Lévi-Strauss' critique of early anthropological approaches to questions of culture and religion.
- Overview of previous approaches to the totemism—the utilitarian approach of J.G. Frazer and Bronislaw Malinowski, the "functionalist" approaches of Emile Durkheim and A.R. Radcliffe-Brown and Sigmund Freud's psychoanalytic interpretation.
- Lévi-Strauss' claim that totemism is evidence of a kind of thought that registers the passage of humanity from nature to culture.
- Introduction to Lévi-Strauss' notion of *bricolage*.

---

ing from Lévi-Strauss' *Totemism* (1991) and *The Savage Mind* (1966), we will suggest that Lévi-Strauss' dramatic re-formulation of the question of totemism formed the opening of a "second front" in Lévi-Strauss' assault on that evolutionary line of thinking that had defined the emergence of social anthropology as a discipline and marked totemism's liquidation as a discrete category of anthropological analysis.

In chapter two we saw how Lévi-Strauss' analysis of kinship began with monogamous marriage—in other words, at the end of a putative sequence of evolutionary stages that had framed the interpretation of ethnographic evidence in the analysis of kinship for early anthropologists such as Lewis Henry Morgan, who had assumed that marriage was a measure of civilization and not a perfectly ubiquitous institution. Totemism, like kinship, was similarly called upon by early anthropologists to legitimize the imaginative reconstruction of a series of stages of human development from totemism to monotheism and from magic to science, in order to make possible the uncovering of the origins of religion. However, just as in *The Elementary Structures of Kinship* the analysis of kinship was re-framed in terms of the transition from nature to culture and synchronic or timeless systems of symbolically encoded relations, so in *Totemism* and *The Savage Mind* the question of totemism is reformulated by Lévi-Strauss as an instance of an allegedly universal problem that all societies face, namely that of "how men perceive, select, intellectually order, and socially structure the similarities and differences in both the natural and cultural realms respectively, and how connections are established between these two orders" (Worsley 2004, 142).

Likewise, in chapter two, we saw that according to Lévi-Strauss, the exchange of women is equivalent to the exchange of messages. Lévi-Strauss similarly assumes that totemism is a system of signs and messages:

> the operative value of the systems of naming and classifying commonly called totemic derives from their formal character: they are codes suitable for conveying messages which can be transposed into other codes, and for expressing messages received by means of different codes in terms of their own system. (Lévi-Strauss 1966, 75–76)

In other words, just as Lévi-Strauss applies insights gleaned from structural linguistics to the analysis of kinship, so those very same insights are re-deployed to address the question of totemism (see Penner 1989, 166–72). As such, Lévi-Strauss re-writes totemism such that it is no longer the origin of society or the origin of religion but rather is an example of an analogical mode of thought (Lévi-Strauss 1966, 263) for the intellectual ordering or classification of the world, and indeed is an instance of "an original logic, a direct expression of the structure of the mind (and behind the mind, probably, of the brain)." (Lévi-Strauss 1991, 90)

The utilitarian hypothesis

Frazer's work on totemism is embedded in evolutionary assumptions about human social and intellectual development. Frazer subscribes to a view of history as a sequence of world-views which predicts the demise of magic and religion as spurious theories of cause and effect that could only hinder humankind's efforts to control nature and assuage its vicissitudes—hence their inevitable displacement by science. In the first volume of *Totemism and Exogamy*—which includes Frazer's original 1887 essay on the subject—we find Frazer anticipating the later arguments of both Durkheim and Lévi-Strauss: he suggests that it is possible to discern "a rudimentary classification of natural objects under heads which bear a certain resemblance to genera, species, etc. This classification is by some Australian tribes extended so as to include the whole of nature" (Frazer 1910, 78; Jones 2005, 84–85). However, this remark is buried amid the mass of evidence and is not pursued or elaborated further. Indeed, in the conclusion Frazer states that

> Considering the far-reaching effects produced on the fauna and flora of a district by the preservation or extinction of a single species of animals or plants, it appears probable that the tendency of totemism to preserve certain species of plants and animals must have largely influenced the organic life of the countries where it has prevailed. (Frazer 1910, 87)

After the 1887 essay on totemism, Frazer committed himself to the development of this utilitarian hypothesis. As such, Frazer argues that the desirable things of nature are classified and then specific human groups are charged with ensuring the abundance of the plant or animal species with which they are identified (Jones 2005, 150–51). Frazer developed this view from his reading of Spencer and Gillen's account of the *intichiuma* ritual of the Arunta aborigines of central Australia where they had observed that the clans would eat the totem object to (magically) acquire its power and to ensure the totem object's future abundance (Jones 2005, 149). (Both Durkheim and Freud would similarly rely on the field work of Spencer and Gillen). According to Frazer, then, totemism is a form of magic, and indeed "an organized and cooperative system...devised to secure for the members of the community...a plentiful supply of all the natural commodities of which they stood in need," while also securing "immunity from all the perils and dangers to which man is exposed in his struggle with nature" (Frazer in Jones 2005, 157).

Malinowski rejected the evolutionary view of history. But, like Frazer, he claims that totemism—as the expression of a highly selective interest in certain species of plant and animal—should be understood in terms of the economic utility of such species to so-called primitive peoples ("the road from…the savage's belly…to his mind is very short" [Malinowski 1984a, 44]) such that "totemism appears…as a blessing bestowed by religion on primitive man's efforts in dealing with his useful surroundings, upon his 'struggle for existence'" (Malinowski 1984a, 47). Yet, the idea that totem objects are chosen because they have some utilitarian or economic significance for certain human groups is difficult to sustain when one has to perform somersaults to argue for the essential utility of wind, mosquitoes or for that matter, vomit (Worsley 2004, 144). Lévi-Strauss' witty riposte to the utilitarian hypothesis—that "natural species are chosen not because they are 'good to eat' but because they are 'good to think'" (Lévi-Strauss 1991, 89)—indicates the path along which our second group of theorists would begin to tread.

Totemism, religion and the origins of reason

According to Morris (1987, 111), Durkheim owes his fundamental idea about religion and its relation to society to the writings of Fustel de Coulanges and W. Robertson Smith. Coulanges' contribution need not detain us—suffice it to say that he attempted to explicate the relationship between particular religious conceptions and specific social institutions. However, Robertson Smith's *Lectures on the Religion of the Semites* (1889) warrants more of our attention as in it he argued that clan totemism was the earliest form of religion.

According to Robertson Smith, totemism consists of a constellation of practices including the naming of clan groups after animals, the belief that the totemic deity is the clan ancestor, that central to totemic worship is the fact that the totem is surrounded by particular prohibitions and that the totemic sacrifice constitutes an effort to achieve communion between the clan and the totemic god. According to Jones (2005, 103), Robertson Smith elaborates an account of totemism and totemic practices that offers a "materialistic foundation not just of more advanced religions, but of some of the most specific and evocative symbols of Christianity, including the idea of atonement, communion and the Eucharist itself." However, according to Evans-Pritchard (1965, 52), "whilst eating of the totem animal could have been the earliest form of sacrifice and the origin of religion, there is no evidence that it was." Nonetheless, Robertson Smith's emphasis on ritual, sacrifice, taboo and on totemism as an originary source of both religion and social solidarity was to be an important influence on the writings of both Durkheim and Freud.

According to Durkheim, society is both beyond and constitutive of the individual. Individuals internalize the norms, rules and conventions particular to a given society or social group at a given point in time. In other words, individuals—according to Durkheim—act, think and feel in terms of broad structures of action, thought and feeling defined by what Durkheim calls the "collective conscience." Further, these structures of acting, thinking and feeling are prior to the individual. Individuals are born into pre-existing societies and these determine or shape individual behaviour. Durkheim calls these structures of acting, thinking and feeling, "social facts" (Durkheim in Thompson 2004, 59–62). Social facts are crystallized in institutions, legal codes, religious observances and so forth and these, according to Durkheim, constitute the proper domain of sociological analysis. According to Durkheim, social facts have a regulative, constraining or coercive power over the individual and originate not in the individual, but in society. Durkheim conceives of religion in much the same fashion: religion for Durkheim is general, objective and obligatory, and likewise belongs to the realm of social facts thus making it amenable to sociological analysis.

In *The Elementary Forms of the Religious Life* Durkheim begins with four ideas originally developed by Robertson Smith namely, that "primitive" religion is a clan cult, that the cult is totemic, that the clan god is the clan itself and finally that totemism constitutes the earliest and most "primitive" form of religion and is as such associated with societies with the "simplest" material culture and social structure (Evans-Pritchard 1965, 56). Moreover, Durkheim claims that religion is not to be explained in terms of its content but functionally, both in terms of the way it organizes the world into separate realms of the sacred and the profane and the manner in which it symbolically relates individuals to the social group to which they belong:

> All known religious beliefs, whether simple or complex, present one common characteristic: they presuppose a classification of all the things, real or ideal, of which men think, into two classes or opposed groups generally designated by two distinct terms which are translated well enough by the words *profane* and *sacred* (*profane*, *sacré*). This division of the world into two domains, the one containing all that is sacred, the other all that is profane, is the distinctive trait of religious thought; the beliefs, myths, dogmas, and legends are either representations or systems of representations which express the nature of sacred things, the virtues and powers which

are attributed to them, or their relations with each other and with profane things…*a religion is a unified set of beliefs and practices relative to sacred things, that is to say, things set apart and forbidden—beliefs and practices which unite one single moral community called a Church, all those who adhere to them.* (Durkheim in Thompson 2004, 111)

Durkheim's analysis essentially reproduces Robertson Smith's claim that the totemic ritual cements the solidarity of the clans objectified in the materiality of the totem object, and indeed the totem is variously described by Durkheim as a "flag," as a "sign" and as a "symbol" (Durkheim in Thompson 2004, 112), such that its ritualized consumption serves to both produce and sustain the moral unity of the clan. Yet Durkheim's argument is not merely the confirmation of Robertson Smith's research, for Durkheim also argues that the totemic object is a representation that acts "as a mediating order whose status derives from the work of interpretation" (Jenks 2003, 31). If, for Kant, the "categories"—space, time, causality—are hard-wired into the very structure of the mind itself, for Durkheim their origin is social and, as such, totemism, or more generally religion— as a kind of intellectual speculation on nature and society—registers the beginning of scientific thought (Jones 2005, 230–32; Durkheim in Thompson 2004, 122–23) that in fact arises from the effervescence and visceral excitation that collective life engenders.

Like Durkheim, Radcliffe-Brown's approach to the question of totemism is broadly "functionalist" in orientation in that he does not seek to understand totemism substantively or in terms of beliefs but rather as a constellation of practices that function to maintain the solidarity and equilibrium of the social group. Radcliffe-Brown defines totemism as that circumstance whereupon "society is divided into groups and there is a special relation between each group and one or more classes of objects that are usually natural species of animals and plants but may occasionally be artificial objects or parts of an animal" (Radcliffe-Brown 1965, 117). Totemic objects are objects that have been accorded what Radcliffe-Brown calls "ritual value" (1965, 123) and he contends that "any object or event which has important effects upon the well-being (material or spiritual) of a society, or anything which stands for or represents any such object or event, tends to become an object of the ritual attitude" (Radcliffe-Brown 1965, 129). Here, Radcliffe-Brown comes perilously close to the utilitarian hypothesis of Frazer and Malinowski. Moreover, it is an extremely vague formulation that can hardly be said to enrich our understanding of why certain plant or animal species come to have such ritual significance. However, in another essay (1958) in which Radcliffe-Brown's argues for the importance of the comparative method in social anthropology, he reaches somewhat more interesting conclusions about the relations between humans and animals. Regarding the stories recounted by Australian aborigines about animals, Radcliffe-Brown relates that

> If we examine some dozens of these tales we find that they have a single theme. The resemblances and differences of animal species are translated into terms of friendship and conflict, solidarity and opposition. In other words the world of animal life is represented in terms of social relations similar to those of human society. (Radcliffe-Brown 1958, 116)

In this account of totemism, Radcliffe-Brown suggests that the key terms are opposition and integration. Totemism ceases to be a form of religion but rather a mode of thought in which nature becomes an object of contemplation for the expression of socio-cultural differences. Nevertheless, Lévi-Strauss' rejection of this second group of theories centres on the broad claim that totemism is a form of religion and their specific failure to account for why plants and animals become objects for identification. Thus, these interpretations are set aside by Lévi-Strauss in favour of the view that totemism is an instance of a mode of thinking that is universal among non-literate peoples and which he calls "savage" or undomesticated thought (see chapter five).

Oedipus and the transition to culture

Freud's writings—broadly understood—offer a theory of the psychological constitution of the individual, a theory of society, a theory of interpretation and a therapeutic practice, all of which rest on a series of unsettling claims about the role of sexual desire in the formation of the self and the primacy of the hidden realm of the unconscious as a determinant of behaviour. Freud's twin concepts of the libido or "pleasure principle" and the instinct of self-preservation and adaptation which Freud terms the "reality principle" constitute the person as a site of conflict and antagonism between the opposed biological or instinctual demands of the body and external, social demands and pressures. Furthermore, Freud claims that civilization is actually founded upon the repression of the pleasure principle. Through ascetic renunciation libidinous energy can be re-channelled and made available for the task of creating culture. This in turn rests on Freud's assumption that the prohibition against incest is universal and that exogamous marriage constitutes the beginning of culture (see chapter two).

In *Totem and Taboo* Freud draws heavily upon the writings of early anthropologists such as Tylor, Frazer, Robertson Smith and Durkheim. Freud also draws from Ernst Haeckel's theory of recapitulation as a means of arguing that the maturation of the individual can be taken to represent the intellectual and moral development of the species, or that phylogeny recapitulates ontogeny, and Lamarck's theory of "inherited characteristics" as a means of conceiving how a founding event—the moment when *homo* becomes *sapiens* (Fox 2004, 161)—can be remembered. As such, Freud tries to link his earlier research on dreams, hysteria and the unconscious to evolutionist discourse about the origins of religion and culture.

In the chapter titled "Animism, Magic and the Omnipotence of Thoughts" Freud explicitly adopts the developmental or evolutionary framework posed by the likes of Tylor and Frazer, namely that human understanding of the world had passed through three distinct stages, specifically magic/animism, religion and science. Freud develops an analogy between the mental lives of so-called savages, children and neurotics through reference to Frazer's thesis that magical acts presuppose a cosmos in which objects that share a likeness and objects that were formerly in contact with one another remain in a relation of secret "sympathy." Both Tylor and Frazer believed magic to be a kind of proto-science. According to Freud, however, magic is not based in rational speculation or empirical observation but rather in an over estimation of the power of thought. As Freud puts it, "the principle governing magic, the technique of the animistic mode of thinking, is the principle of the 'omnipotence of thoughts'" (2003, 99). According to Freud, so-called primitive peoples believe they can manipulate the real world just by thinking about it. Magical thought is not based on faulty reasoning but rather expresses infantile desires and impulses. Thus, magical practices are parallel or akin to, according to the theory of recapitulation, the behaviour of neurotics and infants or young children because just as neurotic behaviour expresses conflicts encountered at an early stage of psychosexual development in which problems and difficulties are solved in the realm of fantasy rather than in reality so the magical or animistic practices of so-called primitives analogously attempt to solve problems in the realm of thought through the positing of idea correspondences. Similarly, among children, fantasy or play is the realm in which problems are mediated and resolved. Freud then suggests that Frazer's three sequential stages of magic, religion and science correspond to the stages of individual psychosexual development, specifically that magic equals narcissism, religion equals object selection (object selection is characterized by dependence on parental authority) and science equals maturity:

> If we are prepared to accept the account given…of the evolution of human views of the universe—an animistic phase followed by a religious phase and this in turn by a scientific one—it will not be difficult to follow the vicis-

situdes of the 'omnipotence of thoughts' through these different phases. At the animistic stage men ascribe omnipotence to *themselves*. At the religious stage they transfer it to the gods but do not seriously abandon it themselves, for they reserve the power of influencing the gods in a variety of ways according to their wishes. The scientific view of the universe no longer affords any room for human omnipotence; men have acknowledged their smallness and submitted resignedly to death. (Freud 2003, 102–103)

The infant, the neurotic and the primitive are thus similar to the extent to which each seeks to satisfy urgent desires and impulses in thought or fantasy rather than in rational action.

In the final chapter titled "The Return of Totemism in Childhood" Freud turns to the Oedipus complex to explain totemism and, borrowing Darwin's notion of the "primal horde," he suggests that the origin of totemism lies in a primal crime. The horde is imagined as human group dominated by a single male or father who prevents the other younger males—his sons—from having any access to the women of the group. One day, the expelled younger males, frustrated by their lack of access to the women of the horde, band together and kill—and then eat—the dominant male or father. (They eat the father, according to Freud, to absorb his strength, potency and power). Later, filled with remorse for what they have done, the sons institute a series of rites and rules at the centre of which is the prohibition against incest enshrined in the rule of exogamous marriage. These rites both repeat and commemorate the original crime, and Freud suggests that the totem is the symbolic substitute for the father. The taboo against killing and eating the totem and the denial of access to the liberated women of the group that the murder brings about sees the institution of totemic religion and exogamy—the basis of civilization and the expression of the repressed desires at the heart of the Oedipus complex, namely to kill the father and to have sexual access to the mother.

In this highly speculative theory, Freud seeks to explain taboo, sacrifice, totemism, religion, exogamy, incest prohibitions and the emergence of culture through recourse to the Oedipus complex. It can also be read as a narrative which states how the rational individual emerges from bonds or relations of domination. Indeed Freud suggests—in "Group Psychology and the Analysis of the Ego"—that the essay be read alongside *Totem and Taboo* (1991, 168). Brickman writes

A juxtaposition of Freud's account of primitivity in *Group Psychology* with that found in *Totem and Taboo* yields a different perspective on his assessment of religion. *Totem and Taboo* mapped an ideological trajectory from animism to religion to rationality and science. *Group Psychology* mapped a political trajectory from embeddedness within group relations marked by emotional thraldom to authority, toward the emergence of the modern subject free from external authority. In both trajectories, the earliest stages are understood as manifestations of an evolutionary primitivity, characterized in *Totem and Taboo* as a belief in animistic illusions, and characterized in *Group Psychology* as a submergence in relations of domination and subjugation. When we join these two trajectories, the primitive illusions of animism and religion emerge as the counterpart to primitive relationships of domination and subordination; the postreligious scientific spirit is the counterpart of the autonomous individual. (Brickman 2003, 147)

This "just-so-story" that is at once myth and history has, it must be said, little if no evidence to support it. Yet in framing his analysis in terms of the opposition nature : culture and in seeking to disclose the principle characteristics of "primitive" thought, one cannot help but note that there is a remarkable convergence in Lévi-Strauss' approach to the question of totemism and that which was initiated by Freud (Fox 2004, 161–162). It now remains for us to delineate the contours of Lévi-Strauss' intervention in the debate about totemism.

The illusion of totemism

Lévi-Strauss' approach to the problem of totemism is summarized by Mendelson as "a matter of classifying classifications" (2004, 119). First, there is the manner in which a given social group classifies or creates taxonomies from its observations of the world. Secondly, there is the way in which different anthropologists or groups of anthropologists have classified the classifications made by those social groups. Thirdly and finally, there is, from a philosophical point of view, the fact that these two activities themselves invite comparison and juxtaposition. We will deal with each of these three points in turn.

In the opening chapter of *The Savage Mind* Lévi-Strauss introduces us to the *bricoleur* (1966, 16), a handy-man or Jacques-of-all-trades working—or in this case thinking—with whatever comes to "hand." The "science of the concrete" (1966, 16) that is the *bricoleur's* stock and trade is rendered as *bricolage*. *Bricolage* is a particular kind of thinking that does not simply impose order on nature, but actually produces nature and culture through the speculative operations of thought. Lévi-Strauss begins with examples of how animals and plants are classified in the taxonomic systems of allegedly primitive peoples and he concludes by saying that "animals and plants are not known as a result of their usefulness; they are deemed to be useful or interesting because they are first of all known" (1966, 9). This surely constitutes a shift in emphasis from *The Elementary*

Structures of Kinship: there, Lévi-Strauss located structure at the level of the unconscious or at the realm of that which is tacit and taken-for-granted. By contrast, in the opening pages of *The Savage Mind* we are confronted with an altogether different realm of knowledge, a realm that is entirely (self)-conscious (Mendelson 2004, 124). Nevertheless, the basic concerns remain the same. Just as in his work on kinship Lévi-Strauss sought to reveal invariant, basic structures that lay behind a positive tumult of ethnographic evidence, so here Lévi-Strauss will seek to demonstrate that the so-called science of the concrete as revealed in totemic systems of classification has a structure that is universal and unchanging. Moreover, just as in his analysis of kinship Lévi-Strauss posed the rule of reciprocity and the exchange of women as a point of transition between nature and culture, so in *The Savage Mind* the entity that comes to mediate between these two poles is the mind itself.

Secondly, then, there is the manner in which Lévi-Strauss positions himself *vis-à-vis* the writings and theories of other anthropologists about totemism. As I have indicated in the preceding pages, Lévi-Strauss rejected the utilitarian hypothesis as a means of explaining why certain social groups choose to identify with certain species of plant or animal. On this point he suggests that "the animal world and that of plant life are not utilized merely because they are there, but because they suggest a mode of thought" (1991, 13). He also rejected the thesis that totemism constitutes the earliest form of religion again in favour of conceiving it as one manifestation of a more generalized or universal phenomenon:

> The alleged totemism is no more than a particular expression, by means of a special nomenclature formed of animal and plant names (in a certain code, as we should say today), which is its sole distinctive characteristic, of correlations and oppositions which may be formalized in other ways, e.g., among certain tribes of North and South America, by oppositions of the type sky/earth, war/peace, upstream/downstream, red/white, etc. The most general model of this, and the most systematic application, is to be found perhaps in China, in the opposition of the two principles of Yang and Yin, as male and female, day and night, summer and winter, the union of which results in an organized totality (*tao*) such as the conjugal pair, the day, or the year. Totemism is thus reduced to a particular fashion of formulating a general problem, viz., how to make opposition, instead of being an obstacle to integration, serve rather to produce it. (Lévi-Strauss 1991, 89)

In the final chapter of *Totemism*, intriguingly entitled "Totemism from Within," Lévi-Strauss suggests that totemism, a problem that has for so long outwitted anthropologists, has been addressed in a far more satisfactory manner by the philosopher Bergson. Lévi-Strauss suggests that the reason for this lies in the fact that Bergson's thinking "presents curious analogies with that of so many so-called primitive peoples" (1991, 97). In what do these "curious analogies" consist? According to Lévi-Strauss, in

> the same desire to apprehend in a total fashion the two aspects of reality... from the same refusal to choose between the two; and from the same effort to see them as complementary perspectives giving on to the same truth.
>
> (1991, 98–99)

Rousseau is similarly called upon as an example of a philosopher who thinks like a "savage." Lévi-Strauss claims that the *Discours sur L'Origine et les Fondements de L'Inégalité Parmi Les Hommes* (1754) is "without doubt the first anthropological treatise in French literature" because in it "Rousseau poses the central problem of anthropology, viz., the passage from nature to culture" (1991, 99). According to Lévi-Strauss, Rousseau marks the beginnings of culture with "the birth of the intellect" (1991, 100) and in particular in the recognition and codification of difference. Specifically,

> it is because man originally felt himself identical to all those like him...that he came to acquire the capacity to distinguish *himself* as he distinguishes *them*, i.e., to use the diversity of species as a conceptual support for social differentiation. (1991, 101)

Totemism, then, as evidence of a "logic operating by means of binary oppositions" (1991, 101), registers humanity's passage from nature to culture—thoughtful reflection on the extant differences between species enables the production of differences (hierarchies) among human groups. The passage from nature to culture is, simultaneously then, the birth of reflexive thought. As such, Lévi-Strauss suggests that Rousseau, in having empathically intuited a mode of thought he could only imagine, was able to reach closer than the early anthropologists to the truth of the totem ultimately because their concern was not to try to "see" the phenomenon from within but rather to (prejudicially) "separate primitive institutions from our own" (1991, 103).

Thirdly, then, we come to the point at which, in *The Savage Mind*, Lévi-Strauss postulates two modes of thought for which nature could become amenable to intellectual enquiry, "one roughly adapted to that of perception and the imagination: the other at a remove from it" (Lévi-Strauss 1966, 15). In chapter five we will return to this *pensée sauvage* to argue that Lévi-Strauss' anthropological writings on totemism and myth constitute a refutation of evolutionist and functionalist thinking in anthropology and the work of Malinowski and Lucien Lévy-Bruhl in particular. Lévi-Strauss will argue that human beings have an innate capacity for the ordering and classification of their worlds and that it is precisely this mode of intellectual activity that is the mark of the human transition from nature to culture and, moreover, there is no God-point from which to declare one mode of classification superior to another.

Summary

In this chapter we examined some competing theories of totemism and explored Lévi-Strauss' intervention in the debate. We can see that Lévi-Strauss addressed the question of totemism in much the same fashion as he approached the question of kinship: to bring order to an apparently conflicting and contradictory mass of ethnographic data through the application of ideas and methods derived from structural linguistics. The consequence of this intervention was the final dissolution of the category "totemism" via a considered refutation of the stage-theory of intellectual development. This was a part of a generalized transition in the anthropology of religion away from evolutionism and a search for the origins of religion towards so-called symbolic approaches. Magic and religion were no longer conceived as theories that ultimately failed empirical tests or lacked predictive power: instead, they would be understood as symbol systems that communicate information.

Chapter 4

Myths without meaning?

> I...claim to show, not how men think in myths, but how myths operate in men's minds without their being aware of the fact and, as I have already suggested, it would perhaps be better to go still further and, disregarding the thinking subject completely, proceed as if the thinking process were taking place in the myths, in their reflection upon themselves and their interrelation. (Claude Lévi-Strauss, *The Raw and the Cooked*)

In this chapter we will focus on a small number of Lévi-Strauss' key essays and texts rather than trying to offer an overview of everything he has written on the subject. As such, we will concentrate on the essays "The Structural Study of Myth" (1993g); "The Story of Asdiwal" (1994e); the first and fourth volumes on myth namely *The Raw and the Cooked: Introduction to a Science of Mythology I* (1992b) and *The Naked Man: Introduction to a Science of Mythology IV* (1981) as well as *Myth and Meaning* (2001). It is in these texts that Lévi-Strauss outlines a structuralist approach to myth,

---

In this chapter:

- Introduction to Lévi-Strauss' approach to myth.
- Lévi-Strauss' critique of alternative approaches to myth and his application of the structural method to their interpretation.
- Lévi-Strauss' juxtaposition of myth and music.
- Lévi-Strauss' interpretation of the Oedipus myth, the story of Asdiwal and an introduction to his interpretation of South American myths on the origins of fire, tobacco and wild pigs in *The Raw and the Cooked: Introduction to a Science of Mythology*.
- Critique and commentary on Lévi-Strauss' approach to myth by Pierre Clastres, Ivan Strenski, Paul Ricoeur and Jacques Derrida.

---

engages in an impassioned defence of that approach, suggests certain affinities between language, myth and music and offers a number of rather cryptic statements about the meaning of myth. However, we will defer any analysis of myth and history to chapter six where we will examine Lévi-Strauss' handling of the question of temporality in terms of his contrast between "hot" and "cold" or "modern" and "primitive" societies. We will also defer—to the same chapter—discussion of Lévi-Strauss' assault on Sartre's historicism in which Lévi-Strauss argues that what "we" in "the West" call history is in fact myth by another name.

If Lévi-Strauss' own writings on myth are somewhat voluminous—necessitating, on our part, some selectivity in focus—those writings have in turn generated a mass of secondary literature by scholars with backgrounds in anthropology, the study of religions, philosophy and literary criticism. Although it will not be possible to do justice to this vast monument of literature for which Lévi-Strauss' structuralist approach to myth has itself become a kind of mythology, we will examine the principal fault lines which this secondary literature has sought to explore and to exploit, with a particular emphasis on Lévi-Strauss' approach to myth and theories of meaning.

Before moving on to scrutinize the particulars of Lévi-Strauss' readings of specific myths, we should begin first of all by situating his approach to myth in general as part of a broader strategy to write against evolutionist theory in anthropology which assumed the fundamental irrationality or unreason of "savage" peoples and which therefore appeared to pose the possibility that so-called primitive thought was incommensurable with modern, scientific thinking—thus rendering the entire anthropological project suspect:

> Prevalent attempts to explain alleged differences between the so-called primitive mind and scientific thought have resorted to qualitative differences between the working processes of the mind in both cases, while assuming that the entities which they were studying remained very much the same. If our interpretation is correct, we are led toward a completely different view—namely, that the kind of logic in mythical thought is as rigorous as that of modern science, and that the difference lies, not in the quality of the intellectual process, but in the nature of things to which it is applied. This is well in agreement with the situation known to prevail in the field of technology: What makes a steel axe superior to a stone axe is not that the first one is better made than the second. They are equally well made, but steel is quite different to stone. In the same way we may be able to show that the same logical processes operate in myth as in science, and that man has always been thinking equally well; the improvement lies, not in an alleged progress of man's mind, but in the discovery of new areas to which it may apply its unchanged and unchanging powers. (Lévi-Strauss 1993g, 230)

As is clear from the above, Lévi-Strauss argues that while we may be able to distinguish—in so-called primitive and modern societies—two distinct modes or styles of thought, the difference between them does not lie in any qualitative measure of reason. Indeed, like totemism, myth is exemplary of a "*logic of the concrete*...which shows us to be closer—rather than farther from—forms of thought very foreign to ours in appearance" (Lévi-Strauss 1994f, 65) and is an example of *la pensée sauvage* that is ultimately concerned with the ordering of the world (Tilley 1990, 21). One consequence of this insistence on the rationality of so-called primitive societies is that our conventional understanding of myth as the opposite of history and therefore as having no factual basis must be placed in brackets. For Lévi-Strauss, then, myth is truth though, as we shall see, this truth will be shown to lie buried beneath the surface, opaque perhaps to all but Lévi-Strauss himself.

Secondly, we will see how mythology comes, for Lévi-Strauss, to occupy a mediatory position between those two poles with which we are by now so familiar, namely, "nature" and "culture." Indeed, Lévi-Strauss will suggest that myth constitutes a realm of thought in and through which contradictions can be posed and resolved—"the purpose of myth is to provide a logical model capable of overcoming a contradiction" (1993g, 229). Here, perhaps, lies Lévi-Strauss' debt to Freud for whom exogamy was, as the denial of the libido or sexual instinct, the beginning of culture and for whom religion was an area of human belief and practice concerned with the mediation of contradictions between the demands of the libido and the so-called reality principle. We might also see here a possible debt to Marx, for whom ideology was that ideational realm in which contradictions could be resolved precisely because they could not be so resolved at the material level. However, it has also been suggested that Lévi-Strauss' approach to myth owes something to Hegel's notion of the dialectic. According to Douglas, "when Lévi-Strauss says that mythic thought follows a strict logic of its own, he means a Hegelian logic of thesis, antithesis, and synthesis" (Douglas 2004, 52). Burridge (2004, 93) argues in similar fashion. However, we should probably be cautious in attributing influences and/or similarities between the likes of Freud, Marx, Hegel and Lévi-Strauss, especially given that when such similarities are asserted, they are usually based in a very narrow reading of both Lévi-Strauss and the comparator.

Thirdly, we should also note the manner in which Lévi-Strauss seeks to establish links and continuities across his studies of kinship, totemism, *la pensée sauvage* and myth. For example, in *The Raw and the Cooked*, Lévi-Strauss claims that "starting from ethnographic experience, I have always aimed at drawing up an inventory of mental patterns, to reduce apparently arbitrary data to some kind of order, and to attain a level at which a kind of necessity becomes apparent, underlying the illusions of liberty" (1992b, 10). Similarly in *Myth and Meaning*, he looks back upon his work on kinship as an effort to "find an order behind…apparent disorder" (2001, 8). Importantly, he suggests that his analyses of various myths should be understood in exactly the same terms.

Language, myth and music

In order to draw out the analogies that Lévi-Strauss claims exist between language, myth and music, we must commence by observing the manner in which Lévi-Strauss characterizes previous approaches to myth—"in order to understand what a myth really is," he writes, "must we choose between platitude and sophism?" (1993g, 207)—and as such seeks to establish the efficacy and scientificity of the structuralist approach. Jung is taken to task for assuming that mythological archetypes have a fixed meaning (1993g, 208). This reproach allows Lévi-Strauss to draw upon Saussure's insight as to the arbitrary nature of the sign which, according to Lévi-Strauss, "was a prerequisite for the accession of linguistics to the scientific level" (1993g, 209). This remark functions, of course, to suggest that (at last) the study of myth can attain a similar level of scientificity. But, if meaning does not reside in "isolated elements" (1993g, 210) where, then, might it be found? According to Lévi-Strauss, meaning resides in the combination of elements—or "mythemes" (1993g, 211)—and in the relations that can be drawn, by the structuralist reader, between them (Penner 1989, 175). Lévi-Strauss, then, fabricates an analogy between language, myth and music as a means of re-imagining Saussure's distinction between the syntagmatic-diachronic and paradigmatic-synchronic dimensions of language (see chapter one):

> Hence the hypothesis: What if patterns showing affinity, instead of being read considered in succession, were to be treated as one complex pattern and read as a whole? By getting at what we call *harmony*, they would then see that an orchestra score, to be meaningful, must be read diachronically along one axis—that is, page after page, from left to right—and synchronically along the other axis, all the notes written vertically making up one gross constituent unit, that is, one bundle of relations.
>
> (Lévi-Strauss 1993g, 212)

We find the juxtaposition of myth and music repeated in the essay "The Story of Asdiwal" (Lévi-Strauss 1994e), where Lévi-Strauss distinguishes between the narrative or syntagmatic-diachronic sequence of events, or "the chronological order in which things happen" (1994e, 161), and various paradigmatic-synchronic levels arranged vertically across which the happenings that the myth recounts, take place. Whereas the former is compared to melody (which proceeds along the syntagmatic-diachronic axis), the latter is compared to "contrapuntal schemata which are vertical" (1994e, 161), again insinuating that the practice of reading (Western) music provides a model for reading myths, in that it is a process that must proceed both horizontally from page to page and vertically from stave to stave at the same time. Lévi-Strauss clarifies the analogy between language, myth and music further in *Myth and Meaning*:

> It is impossible to understand a myth as a continuous sequence. This is why we should be aware that if we try to read a myth as we read a novel or a newspaper article, that is line after line, reading from left to right, we don't understand the myth, because we have to apprehend it as a totality and discover that the basic meaning of the myth is not conveyed by the sequence of events but—if I may say so—by bundles of events although these events appear at different moments in the story. Therefore, we have to read the myth more or less as we would read an orchestral score, not stave after stave, but understanding that we should apprehend the whole page and understand that something which was written on the first stave at the top of the page acquires meaning only if one considers that it is part and parcel of what is written below on the second stave, the third stave, and so on. That is, we have to read not only from left to right, but at the same time vertically, from top to bottom. We have to understand that each page is a totality. And it is only by treating the myth as if it were an orchestral score, written stave after stave, that we can understand it as a totality, that we can extract the meaning out of the myth. (Lévi-Strauss 2001, 40)

This structural harmonics is also central to the comparison of different myths to one another and in the juxtaposition of different versions of the same myth. According to Lévi-Strauss, myths exhibit a "'slated' structure" (1993g, 229), they proliferate in spiral fashion and correspond to a "crystal" forming an "intermediary entity between a statistical aggregate of molecules and the molecular structure itself" (1993g, 229). Thus, in the comparison of differing versions of, say, the Oedipus myth, the repetitive reduplication of specific so-called mythemes across those differing versions functions "to render the structure of the myth apparent" (1993g, 229). Further, in *The Raw and the Cooked* (1992b), Lévi-Strauss claims that he will "treat the sequences of each myth, and the myths themselves in respect of their reciprocal interrelations, like the instrumental parts of a musical work and to study them as one studies a symphony" (1992b, 26). Given that the myths Lévi-Strauss chooses for analysis across the four volumes of the "introduction to a science of mythology" come from both South and North America and as such from different linguistic and cultural groups, the stated aim to treat the myths as a whole is surely both highly significant and controversial. Interestingly, Lévi-Strauss describes *The Raw and the Cooked* (1992b) as proceeding "not along a linear axis but in a spiral" (1992b, 4), as if the work itself has a mythical structure and Lévi-Strauss himself says that his work on myth "is…the myth of mythology" (1992b, 12).

Lévi-Strauss' journey away from previous and what can be summarized as "symbolic" and "functional" approaches to myth (Leach 1970b, 47–48) to structural linguistics—as an example of a science—and then on to music as a means of proposing a structuralist approach to myth actually defines the construction of *The Raw and the Cooked* (1992b), which begins with an "Overture" and continues through a series of "variations," "symphonies," "solos," "fugues" and a "chorus." Indeed, Lévi-Strauss claims that

> there are…groups of myths, which are constructed like a sonata, or a symphony, or a rondo, or a toccata, or any of all the musical forms which music did not invent but borrowed unconsciously from the structure of the myth.
>
> (Lévi-Strauss 2001, 44–45)

This claim is premised on the notion that the emergence of a certain "classical" form of music in the West coincided precisely with the decline of myth:

> There is a period in Western civilization when mythical thinking weakens and disappears to the benefit of novelistic expression. This split takes place in the seventeenth century. Now, at that time, we witness a phenomenon I believe to be intimately connected with the first: the birth of what is called the great musical form, which seems to reiterate the structures of mythical thought. Modes of thought fallen into disuse as a means of expressing the real are still present in the unconscious and seek new employment. Now they no longer articulate meaning but sound. And because of their former use, it is possible for the sounds thus articulated to acquire a meaning for us.
>
> (Lévi-Strauss and Eribon 1991, 177)

Indeed, Lévi-Strauss will even claim that "Wagner is…the undeniable originator of the structural analysis of myths" (Lévi-Strauss 1992b, 15), and in an almost Nietzschean flourish—if we remember that for the early Nietzsche, Wagner's work opened the possibility for the restoration of social bonds despite the murder of God and the emptiness of science—Lévi-Strauss claims that both myth and music "are instruments for the obliteration of time" (1992b, 16), and as we shall see later on in this book, Lévi-Strauss' ambivalent attitude towards time and history is deeply intertwined with a Rousseau-esque nostalgia for societies without history which are, at the same time, societies in which sociality is defined by the authenticity of unmediated presence (see chapter six).

The upshot of these strange allusions and pronouncements is the idea that in order to understand a myth or a constellation of myths, it is not enough—if one wants to know the truth of myth—simply to consider a myth in terms of its immediate socio-historical context, say, for example, as a charter for a particular organization of power and property in a given society, or as an adjunct to ritual practices conceived perhaps as valves for catharsis. Rather, Lévi-Strauss argues that myths, sometimes from disparate regions, can be juxtaposed and compared because they provide their own context for interpretation. Moreover, the juxtaposition and comparison of different myths reveals considerable similarities in the manner in which certain (universal) problems are posed and resolved. Ultimately, as we shall see, this rests in the last analysis upon the assumption that behind all myths lies a single, transcendental signified—the human mind that generates them.

The harmonics of Oedipus

Lévi-Strauss' essay "The Structural Study of Myth" (1993g) begins with the observation that in myth the nature : culture opposition is constantly transgressed. In myth, human beings converse, live with and have sexual relations with animals, reside on land or just as likely in the sky or the sea and perform magical acts as a matter of course. However, Lévi-Strauss claims that despite the apparent variety if not tumult and chaos that confronts the student of myth, a deep and hidden meaning will be revealed if we go about the analysis in the right way:

> Mythology confronts the student with a situation which at first sight appears contradictory. On the one hand it would seem that in the course of a myth anything is likely to happen. There is no logic, no continuity. Any characteristic can be attributed to any subject; every conceivable relation can be found. With myth, everything becomes possible. But on the other hand, this apparent arbitrariness is belied by the astounding similarity between myths collected in widely different regions. Therefore the problem: If the content of a myth is contingent, how are we going to explain the fact that myths throughout the world are so similar? (Lévi-Strauss 1993g, 208)

As such, Lévi-Strauss proposes an analysis of the Oedipus myth. He disassembles the text into events or segments along the syntagmatic-diachronic chain that refer to relationships between characters and entities of differing status, and identifies the following eight events or segments (1993g, 214):

i) Cadmos seeks his sister Europe, ravished by Zeus;

ii) Cadmos kills the dragon;

iii) The Spartoi—men born from the sowing of a dragon's teeth—kill one another;

iv) Oedipus kills his father, Laios;

v) Oedipus kills the Sphinx;

vi) Oedipus marries his mother, Jocasta;

vii) Eteocles kills his brother, Polynices;

viii) Antigone buries her brother Polynices despite having being ordered not to by her uncle, Creon.

Lévi-Strauss also draws his reader's attention to the meaning of three of the mythical characters' names:

i) Labdacos, Laios' father, means "lame;"

ii) Laios, Oedipus' father, means "left-sided;"

iii) Oedipus means "swollen-footed."

Lévi-Strauss then re-orders the eleven events or segments into four columns which are variously described as 'mythemes', 'gross constituent units' and 'bundles of relations'. Note the violence being done to the telling of the myth—we are no longer interested in the syntagmatic-diachronic unfolding of the myth as it is told in time but in the structural relations that the myth encodes between the mythemes. Thus, the four columns below represent the paradigmatic-synchronic harmonics of the myth:

I	II	III	IV
Cadmos–Europe	Spartoi	Cadmos–Dragon	Lame–Labdacos
Oedipus–Jocasta	Oedipus–Laios	Oedipus–Sphinx	Left-sided–Laios
Antigone–Polynices	Eteocles–Polynices		Swollen-footed–Oedipus

In the first column Lévi-Strauss places those incidents that are comparable to incest in that they can be characterized as the "over-rating of blood relations." In column two we find a significant contrast being drawn—here the incidents or segments are comparable to fratricide and parricide in that they can be characterized as the "under-rating of blood relations." Columns one and two, then, form a binary pair or opposition. In column three we find the destruction of anomalous monsters by human beings and in column four we find references to human beings who are in some sense themselves anomalous. According to Lévi-Strauss, it is a universal feature of mythological accounts of men born from the earth that they should have problems walking straight or upright. Furthermore, the monsters in column three are half-human and half-animal while the sowing of the dragon's teeth which in turn leads to the birth of the Spartoi implies the doctrine of the autochthonous origins of human beings—the Spartoi were born from the earth growing like plants. Similarly, the story that Oedipus had been staked to the ground at birth—hence his swollen foot—implies that even though he was born of a woman he was not fully separated from the earth. Thus Lévi-Strauss claims that just as the first two columns form a binary opposition or pair, so too do columns three and four: column three, in which anomalous monsters are killed, signifies the denial of the autochthonous origins of human beings while column four signifies the persistence of the idea of the autochthonous origins of human beings (1993g, 215–16). According to Lévi-Strauss, then, the myth constitutes an attempt to mediate and resolve aspects of humankind's transition from nature to culture:

> The myth has to do with the inability, for a culture which holds the belief that mankind is autochthonous...to find a satisfactory transition between this theory and the knowledge that human beings are actually born from the union of man and woman. Although the problem obviously cannot be solved, the Oedipus myth provides a kind of logical tool which relates the original problem—born from one or born from two?—to the derivative problem: born from different or born from the same? By a correlation of this type, the overrating of blood relations is to the underrating of blood relations as the attempt to escape autochthony is to the impossibility to succeed in it. Although experience contradicts theory, social life validates cosmology by its similarity of structure. Hence cosmology is true. (Lévi-Strauss 1993g, 216)

La geste de Lévi-Strauss

The story of Asdiwal is in fact a series of myths related by the Tsmishian peoples—migratory hunters and fishers who live on the Pacific coast, south of Alaska. The migrations of game and fish dictate the peregrinations of the Tsimshian, who move from the sea to the mountains along the Nass and Skeena rivers. Like other peoples in the same region, the Tsimshian do not practice agriculture. During the summer months the women collect fruit, berries, plants and roots while the men hunt bears and goats in the mountains and sea-lions on the coast. They also practice deep-sea fishing for cod and halibut, but they also fish for herring closer to shore and for fresh-water fish along the two rivers. At the end of winter, they often experience hunger as their supplies of food frequently run dangerously low. Important too is the fact that the Tsimshian are organized in matrilineal clans which are exogamous and are themselves divided into lineages, descent lines and households (Lévi-Strauss 1994e, 147–49).

In his analysis of the story of Asdiwal, Lévi-Strauss identifies four levels to the myth: geographical, economic, sociological and cosmological. In other words, the myth deals with the reality of hunger and of forced migration in search of game. It also deals with kinship, marriage residence and beliefs about gods and other realms of existence. Lévi-Strauss then identities five schemas: first, a "geographical schema" in which Asdiwal journeys from east to west and west to east, with the return journey incorporating a south–north–north–south movement which corresponds to the migrations of the Tsimshian on the rivers Nass and Skeena in their search for food; second, a "cosmological schema" in which Asdiwal journeys to heaven and a subterranean realm; third, an "integration schema" in which the complementarity of the previous two schemas is demonstrated; fourth, a "sociological schema" in which Asdiwal's marital adventures are said to describe a process whereby patri-local residence gives way steadily to matri-local residence before returning again to patri-local residence and fifth, a "techno-economic schema" in which Lévi-Strauss notes the fact that the myth begins with famine and ends with a successful hunt. Lévi-Strauss, then, juxtaposes the initial and final states of affairs described in the myth to draw up the following table of oppositions: female : male, east-west : high-low, famine : repletion and movement : immobility (Lévi-Strauss 1994e, 162–64). "Having separated out the codes," writes Lévi-Strauss, "we have analysed the structure of the message. It now remains to decipher the meaning" (Lévi-Strauss 1994e, 162–65). The final "meaning" of the myth turns out to be related to rules of marriage and residence and the (ideological?) legitimation of one state of affairs above and over other possible states:

> Mythical speculations about types of residence which are exclusively patrilocal or matrilocal do not…have anything to do with the reality of the structure of Tsimshian society, but rather with its inherent possibilities and latent potentialities. Such speculations, in the last analysis, do not seek to depict what is real, but to justify the shortcomings of reality, since the extreme positions are only imagined in order to show that they are untenable…This conception of the relation of the myth to reality no doubt limits the use of the former as a documentary source. But it opens the way for other possibilities; for, in abandoning the search for a constantly accurate picture of ethnographic reality in the myth, we gain, on occasions, a means of reaching unconscious categories. (Lévi-Strauss 1994e, 173)

It is the final refrain of the above that marks out the difference between a fairly orthodox Marxist account of myth-as-ideology and as a legitimacy charter for a particular state of social affairs and Lévi-Strauss' account: for our putative Marxist, "unconscious categories" would be the product of historically necessary forces, whereas for Lévi-Strauss they are biologically hard-wired into the structure of the mind and are as such immanent in cultural products such as myth.

The raw and the cooked

In the first volume of his "introduction to the science of mythology," Lévi-Strauss details a number of myths which recount the origins of fire, the origins of wild pigs and the origins of tobacco, and demonstrates their inter-relatedness. Thus, in Kayapo and Bororo myths that detail the origins of fire (Lévi-Strauss 1992b, 66–78), we find that the myths commonly refer to a time when human beings had not mastered the use of fire, and so warmed their meat by leaving it on stones under the sun. The knowledge of fire is attributed to a jaguar which rescues the hero, gives him a magic bow and arrows and adopts him as his own son. However, the jaguar's wife is unhappy with this arrangement (a crucial detail of this myth is that, according to Lévi-Strauss, the jaguar is married to a human wife. However, according to Maybury-Lewis [1970, 156] the jaguar's wife is also a jaguar). She is killed by the hero who then returns home and passes on what he has learned of fire to his village. Lévi-Strauss notes that jaguars and humans constitute a binary opposition: one eats raw meat the other cooked; the jaguar eats people but people do not east jaguars. According to Lévi-Strauss, "between the two opposite poles exists a relation based on a total absence of reciprocity" (1992b, 83). It is the jaguar's wife that mediates between the two extremes opening the possibility that human beings can acquire from the jaguar the means to hunt and the means to cook their food. Once this has happened she serves no further purpose and can thus be eliminated, thus returning jaguars and human beings to a condition characterized by the absence of reciprocity, but with jaguars and human beings having changed places.

In myths that recount the origins of wild pigs, the hero travels to the earth and entrusts the care of his god-son with some villagers where some relatives of his god-child live. The villagers are negligent and, on the hero's return, the boy complains of his maltreatment. The hero surrounds the village with feathers and sets them ablaze. The trapped villagers, in a state of confusion, engage in unrestrained sexual activity and their cries of pleasure become grunts until they are finally transformed into wild pigs.

They remain in the village/pigsty until a rival of the hero releases them into the forest.

According to Lévi-Strauss, there is a symmetry between the myths that recount the origins of fire and the myths that recount the origins of wild pigs in that they function to code relations between affines and kin. The jaguar is like a benevolent brother-in-law who, in exchange for the wife he has received offers knowledge of fire, whereas the pigs are the equivalent of the malevolent brother-in-law, who shirks his obligations. Lévi-Strauss thus suggests that on one level the myths encode aspects of kinship and, at a deeper level, they encode the basic opposition of nature : culture. On the level of kinship relations and obligations, wife-takers are represented as

> Jaguars or wild pigs: jaguars, when nature is tending in the direction of culture, since the jaguar is a brother-in-law who behaves with civility and presents man with the arts of civilization; pigs, when culture is degenerating into nature, the wild pigs being former human beings who behaved coarsely, and who, instead of improving the daily diet of their brothers-in-law…promptly settled down to sexual enjoyment—in other words, were takers on a natural level instead of being givers on the cultural level.
> (Lévi-Strauss 1992b, 94)

On the deeper level of the opposition of nature to culture, Lévi-Strauss notes that

> The…myths…about the origin of fire…function in terms of a double contrast: on the one hand, between what is raw and what is cooked, and on the other, between the fresh and the decayed. The raw/cooked axis is characteristic of culture; the fresh/decayed one of nature, since cooking brings about cultural transformation of the raw, just as putrefaction is its natural transformation. (Lévi-Strauss 1992b, 142)

Lévi-Strauss then moves on to demonstrate that a number of apparently distinct myths collected from different South American minority peoples are actually interrelated. As such, the myths about the origins of fire, the origins of wild pigs and the origins of tobacco are linked or better, are "variations" or transformations of one another: (i) tobacco smoke engenders wild pigs which supply meat; (ii) fire is obtained from the jaguar; (iii) to get rid of the jaguar, its corpse is burnt causing the birth of tobacco (1992b, 107).

The audacity of the enterprise is inspired though we may be tempted to see "the oppositions posited between the different 'bundles' of relations… as more of Lévi-Strauss' own, peculiar interpretation of the myth than a disclosure of its essential meaning" (Johnson 2003, 91; see also Gellner 1986, 156). The vast amount of material covered and the shocking and quite brilliant analysis leaves one breathless, and it would be disingenuous of me to leave the impression that justice could be done in just a few pages: the intrigued reader must go to the primary sources and read them for him or herself (see Penner 1989, 177–78). Nevertheless, Lévi-Strauss' approach to myth has generated considerable criticism which usually follows either one of two lines of attack: first, critiques which argue that myths must be understood in terms of their specific socio-cultural and historical context, and cannot be treated as a *sui generis* phenomena; secondly, critiques which accuses Lévi-Strauss of gross reductionism, particularly with regard to the meaning of myth. I shall take each of these lines of attack in turn.

The autonomy of myth

According to Clastres (1994b), Lévi-Strauss' structuralist approach to myth is akin to a "sociology without society" (1994b, 130) because it fails to take seriously the rapport of myth with its immediate socio-historical context. Regardless of whether we have any sympathy for Clastres' argument, it does at the very least encourage us to think carefully about the relationships between texts—written or oral, ideas, and a social formation. Are texts and ideas to be understood as epiphenomena, products whose compass is determined or at least conditioned by a particular organization of power and property in a putative society, or, can texts and ideas be ascribed greater autonomy such that they can be analysed without reference to the society which produced them? Lévi-Strauss makes constant references to the kinship practices of the minority peoples from which the myths were compiled, suggesting indeed that he is always quite careful to read the myth in terms of certain, if pre-selected particulars of

---

Some critical questions:

- Does Lévi-Strauss' assertion of the autonomy of myth assure the objectivity of structuralist analysis, or is it a political strategy for neutralizing myths as potential vehicles for ideology?
- Can texts be studied without reference to any socio-cultural context?
- What is the meaning of myths and mythic symbols? Do myths point to some transcendent sacred? Do they point to the structuring activities of the pan-human mind from which they sprang? Do they mean anything at all?

---

the society that generated it. However, his insistence on the separation and separateness of myth and ritual, the break his approach inscribes with Malinowski's claim that "myth serves principally to establish a sociological charter" (Malinowski 1984b, 144) and the emphasis on comparative analysis in order to elucidate something beyond and behind any immediate socio-historical context suggests not only the reduction of myth to a formal logic stripped bare of any emotional or affective dimensions but also—as Strenski (1987) observes—an attempt to render myth "invulnerable to appropriation by political and emotional primitivists" (1987, 162).

According to Strenski, "the other side of…structuralism" (1987, 163) is a hatred for "romanticism" and "primitivism"—not only then "hatred" for evolutionary anthropology which fetishized so-called primitives in a search for its own origins but also for political myths and the likes of Mircea Eliade whose writings on myth and whose early commitments to fascism constitute an interesting and uncomfortable conjunction, especially given his enormous influence in the study of religions (Eliade 1959; but see McCutcheon 1997). However, by "seeing one myth as simply a variant in a set of structural transformations" (Strenski 1987, 168), myths, in the hands of Lévi-Strauss, are relativized and seem to lose their potential to function as political vehicles or weapons, though elsewhere Lévi-Strauss has claimed that a myth is like a grid of intelligibility that "confers meaning… on the images of the world, of the society and of its history" (Lévi-Strauss 1985d, 145), suggesting that the chain of myths, charters and ideology is a difficult one to break. We might, then, be tempted to read Lévi-Strauss' insistence on the autonomy of myth not as a sign of the scientificity of the structuralist approach but rather as a strategy for writing against fascist, Stalinist and nationalist mythologies—ideologies—where places and peoples and imagined destinies are woven together for the purpose of harnessing and mobilizing allegedly preternatural energies towards political objectives. Given the horrors of the twentieth century—which we seem to be perpetuating with remarkable enthusiasm and abandon as we get into the twenty-first—Lévi-Strauss' attempt to dis-articulate myth from politics and his effort to assert the autonomy of myth, surely demonstrates that the attempt to give the study of myth a scientific footing is indeed a political strategy. The language of the laboratory, of disinterested, scientific observation and of objectivity—indeed, the language of structuralism—is then perhaps revealed as a distinct genre of polemic that consciously seeks to mask its own partisan and political nature. We will have more to say about Lévi-Strauss' politics in chapter six.

Myths without meaning?

What does it mean, "to mean?" In everyday talk about meaning, we tend to frame the verb "to mean" in terms of some subjective sense we believe we give, as individuals, to our speaking and writing. Our presence to meaning is meaning's guarantee (the circle is clearly vicious). For Clifford Geertz—an anthropologist who wrote a great deal about religion and who, moreover, positioned himself against structuralism arguing that the study of culture is not "an experimental science in search of law, but an interpretive one in search of meaning" (Geertz 1973, 5)—human beings endow their actions with meaning. This is, according to Geertz, the essential and defining characteristic of human being. It is these subjective meanings that anthropology in its interpretive variant seeks to access and then frame in terms of local meaning systems.

Phenomenological and hermeneutic approaches to myth and religion similarly seek to access what it is that believer's intend, think or believe. For example, Maurice Leenhardt—who occupied the chair in comparative religion at the Ecole Pratique des Hautes Etudes before Lévi-Strauss' election in 1950—argued that anthropological analysis ought to begin phenomenologically, by privileging the "native" point of view and by inviting said natives to interpret their own practices and beliefs (Strenski 1987, 141). However, Lévi-Strauss suggests that this leaves half of the work of anthropological analysis undone:

> Ethnographers tend to believe too readily that they have succeeded in grasping, beyond their own preconceptions, the ideas of the indigenous people. Their descriptions are too often reduced to a phenomenology. We hope to introduce an additional exigency into our disciplines: to discover, beyond men's idea of their society, the hinges of the "true" system. We hope to carry the investigation beyond the limits of consciousness.
>
> (Lévi-Strauss 1994f, 67)

Given the above, when Lévi-Strauss talks about meaning we must take him to "mean" something quite different. Indeed, Lévi-Strauss accuses contemporary philosophy of being "imbued with…mysticism" (Lévi-Strauss 1981, 645) because it wants "mythology to be full of hidden meaning" (1981, 646):

> They hold it against me that the extra meaning I distil from the myths is not the meaning they would have liked to find there. They refuse to recognize and to accept the fact of their deafness to the great anonymous voice whose utterance comes from the beginning of time and the depths of the mind. (Lévi-Strauss 1981, 640)

Whereas, in traditional hermeneutics, the meaning of a text or an utterance is to be located in the intentions of a putative speaker or author—intentions that can be accessed through phenomenological empathy and intuition—according to Lévi-Strauss, myths are not authored in any conventional sense. We may say that they have no author and therefore, according to the methods of traditional hermeneutics, they must be meaningless. For example, Paul Ricoeur has argued for the non-arbitrary nature of the religious symbol claiming that that within such symbols can be found "the trace of a natural relationship between the signifier and the signified" (Ricoeur 1974, 319). Ricoeur's argument is founded upon a contrast between the supposed meaning-abundance of the symbol and the assumed meaning-poverty of the sign, and he suggests that such an assumption can augur "new contact with the sacred, a movement beyond the forgetfulness of Being which is today manifested in the manipulation of empty signs and formalized languages" (Ricoeur 1974, 319). But Lévi-Strauss does not say that myths are without meaning: at the end of *The Raw and the Cooked*, Lévi-Strauss argues that the realm of myth constitutes a "matrix of meanings":

> Each matrix of meanings refers to another matrix, each myth to other myths. And if it is now asked to what final meaning these mutually significant meanings are referred—since in the last resort and in their totality they must refer to something—the only reply to emerge from this study is that myths signify the mind that evolves them by making use of the world of which it is itself a part. Thus there is simultaneous production of myths themselves, by the mind that generates them and, by the myths, of an image of the world which is already inherent in the structure of the mind.
> (Lévi-Strauss 1992b, 340–41)

According to Lévi-Strauss, then, meaning resides not in some emotionally charged symbol but rather signifies an organizing principle that lies behind all the products of human culture:

> What does 'to mean' mean? It seems to me that the only answer we can give is that 'to mean' means the ability of any kind of data to be translated in a different language...Now, what would a translation be without rules? It would be absolutely impossible to understand. Because you cannot replace any word by any other word or any sentence by any other sentence, you have to have rules of translation. To speak of rules and to speak of meaning is to speak of the same thing; and if we look at all the intellectual undertakings of mankind...the common denominator is always to introduce some kind of order. (Lévi-Strauss 2001, 9)

In myth, then, it is the mind that is revealed, and in Lévi-Strauss' approach to myth we are confronted with mind narcissistically contemplating itself (Merquior 1988, 54).

Well, not quite. At other moments, Lévi-Strauss not only says that "myths are anonymous" (1992b, 18) but also that they come "from nowhere" (1992b, 18). Moreover, he writes "if it is…asked where the real centre of the work is to be found, the answer is that this is impossible to determine" (1992b, 17) and that "in everything I have written on mythology I have wanted to show that one never arrives at a final meaning" (Lévi-Strauss and Eribon 1991, 142). As Derrida notes, Lévi-Strauss, in his treatment of myth, abandons "all reference to a *centre*, to a *subject*, to a privileged *reference*, to an *origin*, or to an absolute *archia*" (Derrida 2002, 361). Lévi-Strauss is, all of a sudden, a post-structuralist to the extent that myths-as-signifiers point not to any source, ground, or foundation but only to other myths-as-signifiers in an endless chain in and through which meaning, like tobacco smoke, always on the edge of substantiality, seems to approach solidity before melting into air.

Summary

In this chapter I have outlined Lévi-Strauss' approach to myth. If in his analyses of kinship and totemism it was a matter of reducing a mass of ethnographic data to some kind of order, in his analysis of myth it is the myths themselves that are subject to this process of reduction and re-ordering. At this point we may wonder whether this propensity to order is a universal facet of the human mind or rather simply a contingent aspect of Lévi-Strauss' own approach to anthropology.

I have also referred to the observations of Clastres (1994b), Strenski (1987), Ricoeur (1974) and Derrida (2002) to highlight some points of departure for a critique of Lévi-Strauss' approach to myth. From the point of view of the study of religions, we should note the severity of the break between the substantive or "meaning-laden" approach to (mythic) symbols pursued by the likes of Jung and Eliade (Ellwood 1999, 171) and the relational or structuralist approach elaborated by Lévi-Strauss.

Chapter 5

Structuralism, shamanism and material culture

This thirst for objective knowledge is one of the most neglected aspects of the thought of people we call 'primitive.' Even if it is rarely directed towards facts of the same level as those with which modern science is concerned, it implies comparable intellectual application and methods of observation. In both cases the universe is an object of thought at least as much as it is a means of satisfying needs. Every civilization tends to overestimate the objective orientation of its thought and this tendency is never absent. When we make the mistake of thinking that the Savage is governed solely by organic or economic needs, we forget that he levels the same reproach at us and that to him his own desires for knowledge seems more balanced than ours. (Claude Lévi-Strauss, *The Savage Mind*)

In this chapter we will be concerned in the first instance with a single text—*The Savage Mind* (1966)—as a means of picking out the threads of continuity across Lévi-Strauss' writings on kinship, totemism and myth. Thus, the first half of this chapter will constitute a pause, a moment for reflection for the purpose of looking back across the seemingly disparate and diverse territories we have traversed. However, it will also provide us an opportunity to see what is ahead of us, for *The Savage Mind* is

> **In this chapter:**
> - Introduction to *The Savage Mind* and the essays on shamanism and art.
> - Introduction to Lévi-Strauss' terms including *la pensée sauvage*, the *bricoleur*, *bricolage* and the critique of early anthropological approaches to questions of culture and religion.
> - Lévi-Strauss' naturalist explanation of cultural and religious symbol systems.
> - From culture to ideology: Lévi-Strauss' essays on shamanism, political authority and Caduveo art.

© Equinox Publishing Ltd. 2008, Unit 6, The Village, 101 Amies Street, London SW11 2JW an odd and perhaps even a faintly schizophrenic book—Lévi-Strauss will engage some familiar adversaries and in particular the evolutionist assumptions of the early anthropologists who asserted the essential irrationality of so-called primitive thinking: it resembles his previous writings on kinship and totemism in that it is not based on Lévi-Strauss' own field work but rather constitutes a critical re-reading of the anthropological canon that effectively reframes how that canon, and the evidence laid forth within it, is to be interpreted. As such, Lévi-Strauss juxtaposes ethnographic instances from every corner of the world much like Frazer, an anthropologist whose notoriety today rests entirely on the fact that he rarely left his armchair.

However, *The Savage Mind* is also partly a polemical work, written not only in the style of the cool and detached observer who writes for a narrow audience of specialists, but also in the style of an engaged and passionate public intellectual. We will only note the existence of that other Lévi-Strauss here, but we shall get to know it better in the following chapter. For the time being we will explore Lévi-Strauss' notions of *la pensée sauvage* and *bricolage* to see first how they take us, paradoxically, not to culture but to nature and culture's biological basis in the structure of the human mind and secondly, to a species of relativism.

We shall also—through reference to an anecdote Lévi-Strauss relates in *Tristes Tropiques* (1992a) which is connected to a wider discussion about political authority among the South American minority peoples with whom he did his field work, and two essays on shamanism titled "The Sorcerer and his Magic" (1993h) and "The Effectiveness of Symbols" (1993i)— highlight the fact that Lévi-Strauss is not a consistent structuralist. In these essays we will see Lévi-Strauss drawing parallels between shamanism and psychoanalysis. Finally, we will briefly review Lévi-Strauss' analysis of Caduveo art in which a strict structuralist analysis is again rejected in favour of a more conventionally sociological explanation.

La pensée sauvage et le bricoleur

In the first chapter of *The Savage Mind* Lévi-Strauss initiates an analysis of what he calls "the science of the concrete" through distinguishing between "magic" on the one hand, and "science" on the other. Perhaps inevitably, such a discussion is reminiscent of debates among evolutionist anthropologists such Frazer and Tylor and as such, Lévi-Strauss runs the risk of re-inscribing categories he is actually seeking to problematize and take apart. We are invited to consider the fact that so-called primitive peoples have a vast knowledge of nature in order to disprove the assumption of "the intellectual poverty of savages" (1966, 1), and to assume, contrary to Malinowski who suggested that such local knowledge is motivated by the needs of the stomach rather than the brain, that local taxonomies and schemes of classification are "founded on...[a] demand for order" (1966, 10), for any system of ordering, according to Lévi-Strauss, is preferable to chaos (1966, 15). Yet the invocation of Tylor's "primitive philosopher" (1966, 12) and Frazer's opposition of magic to science forces Lévi-Strauss' hand: "I am not however commending a return to the popular belief... according to which magic is a timid and stuttering form of science," rather "it is... better... to compare them as two parallel modes of acquiring knowledge" (1966, 13).

We are also asked to dismiss any notion of stages of intellectual development and to imagine instead "two strategic levels at which nature is accessible to scientific enquiry: one roughly adapted to that of perception and the imagination: the other at a remove from it" (1966, 15). Despite first appearances, then, this is not a return to early theory in anthropology, but a critique of that theory which must nevertheless work with as well as against the categories that were employed to organize the evidence marshalled in support of the evolutionary hypothesis.

Nevertheless, we might legitimately ask a question regarding the use of the word *sauvage*, which has been translated into English as "savage." Certainly, the word "savage" can only serve to remind us of certain sometimes racially motivated prejudices about peoples and cultures we once called "primitive." But in French the word connotes a number of other associations as well including that which is "wild," "untamed," "natural" and "spontaneous" (Caws 1970, 200). As such, *la pensée sauvage*—savage thought—is supposed to refer not to a previous stage of intellectual and/ or socio-cultural development and nor to a mode of thought distant and inferior to our own as in Lévy-Bruhl's notion of a "pre-logical mentality" where the so-called primitive is irretrievably enmeshed in a web of "mystical participations" (Lévi-Strauss 1966, 38 and 1966, 268; but see Evans-Pritchard 1965, 78–99) (if the distance between magic and science—as worldviews and ways of thinking—is over-emphasized as with Lévy-Bruhl, the very possibility of anthropology is negated or at the very least thrown seriously into doubt. This is why Tylor for one argued for the psychic unity of humanity, and indeed Tylor's mode of imaginative reconstruction— memorably described by Evans-Pritchard as an example of the "'if I was horse,' fallacy" [Evans-Pritchard 1965, 24]—is premised precisely on this unity). Instead, Lévi-Strauss conjures the image of the *bricoleur* or odd-job-person who thinks with what is ready-to-hand.

But, how can this invocation of the *bricoleur* and thereafter of *bricolage* as a mode of intellectual assembly, help us access the kinds of intellectual processes that lie behind totemic systems of classification, mythical thinking, magic and religion? Lévi-Strauss juxtaposes his *bricoleur* with an engineer as a means of contrasting the means by which these two persons of craft, think. Thus, the *bricoleur* works with "signs" while the engineer with "concepts" (1966, 20); the *bricoleur* works with "the remains and debris of events," and "is imprisoned in the events and experiences which it never tires of ordering and re-ordering in its search for meaning" to which Lévi-Strauss adds, is a kind of protest "against the idea that anything can be meaningless" (1966, 22), an idea to which science has always, according to Lévi-Strauss, been resigned. As such, totemism and myth are to be understood as special instances of *bricolage* and of *la pensée sauvage*, and in a critique of Comte (1966, 219–20) it is claimed that the thought we have been wont to describe in the most pejorative of terms lives on in our own society particularly in the realm of art. Thus, that way of thinking which at first sight appears strange and unrecognizable, distant both in time and space from the allegedly civilized and modern West, is transformed by Lévi-Strauss into a manner of thinking that though different from scientific thinking—"one is supremely concrete, the other supremely abstract; one proceeds from the angle of sensible qualities and the other from the angle of formal properties" (1966, 269)—cannot be regarded as inferior. While Lévi-Strauss has made the most of a special point of view afforded by his bringing together of structural linguistics and social anthropology—a point of view that he believes is able to "see" both from within and from the outside the essential qualities and properties of *la pensée sauvage*—there is nevertheless no Archimedean point from which to pronounce value-judgements as to the status or worth of so-called primitive thought. Critically, this is because Lévi-Strauss seeks to demonstrate that cultural systems can be reduced to binary oppositions, and that cultural differences can be understood as different mediations or permutations of a basic binary opposition, namely that of nature and culture. The ultimate reduction lies in the contention that the reducibility of cultures into systems actually reflects the binary structure of the mind, a structure that is biologically given and thus natural. Culture is, then, eminently natural. However, our ideas about nature are, at the same time, mediated and indeed produced by culture:

> These two conceptions [nature and culture] stand in a relation of considerable tension. The uniqueness of humanity resides in culture, that which is not natural but socially constructed. However, the basis for this construction is ultimately to be discovered in nature: the cultural is natural. Relations existing in nature are used to produce cultural products which themselves

incorporate those relations. As opposed to this, Lévi-Strauss also stresses at a number of points in his work that a contrast between nature and culture is itself a product of culture. The cultural defines and creates the natural in various forms. (Tilley 1990, 22)

If we are looking for a general theory of religion, we may perhaps at this point find ourselves experiencing the early pangs of disappointment. After-all, "religion" is a word Lévi-Strauss barely deigns to mention. His work on totemism effectively removed it "from the narrow framework of magic and religion and place[d] it within the broader framework of taxonomical activity" (Zimmerman 1970, 220–21). Likewise, his study of myth severs them from any romantic notion of the sacred and instead they too are analyzed as instances of an anonymous mind that thinks in a binary code, like a computer. In both cases, we witness "the reduction of the individual and collective experience of religion to their cognitive dimension" (Johnson 2003, 104). And yet, his notions of *bricolage* and *la pensée sauvage* which are applied as a means to interpret and explain the practices and products of so-called primitive cultures and in the methodology elaborated by Lévi-Strauss for the analysis of myths—which can surely be applied to any kind of text—it would be churlish of us to ignore the fact that Lévi-Strauss has developed sophisticated and challenging arguments against those who would proclaim the fundamental irrationality of non-literate peoples and indeed of magical and religious beliefs and practices. It would also be rash if we were to assume, at this point, that we have covered the essentials both of Lévi-Strauss' thought in general and his work on religions in particular. Chapter six is precisely oriented towards a discussion of what might loosely be termed as Lévi-Strauss' political writings. For the remainder of this chapter we will examine an anecdote from *Tristes Tropiques* (1992a) and the essays on shamanism, "The Sorcerer and his Magic" (1993h) and "The Effectiveness of Symbols" (1993i), where Lévi-Strauss draws out an analogy between shamanism and psychoanalysis, and his analysis of Caduveo body art. In these analyses we will see Lévi-Strauss move away from his usual formalism.

Shamanism, ideology and psychoanalysis

In chapter one, we noted the rather ambiguous relation that holds between Lévi-Strauss and Marx. On the one hand, Lévi-Strauss has spoken of Marx as a major influence on his own thinking. On the other, Lévi-Strauss' borrowings from Marx are almost entirely formal rather than substantive. Importantly, it should by now be clear that Lévi-Strauss' focus on culture and in particular on forms of thought has entirely excluded any discussion

---

Some key terms:

- J.G. Frazer and Lucien Lévy-Bruhl distinguished between magic and science as forms of thought, with science privileged as superior.
- Lévi-Strauss uses the idea of *la pensée sauvage* to designate a mode of thought or way of thinking pervasive among non-literate peoples that ultimately points to the structuring activity of the mind.
- Lévi-Strauss also uses the term *bricolage* to describe this mode of thought as a way of putting things together.
- The term *bricoleur* means odd-job-person and is used to describe this style of thought as a kind of thinking with whatever comes to hand.

---

or analysis of institutions, authorizing practices, socio-political relationships, gender hierarchies or the problem of power. Even where certain issues of this type are broached—such as in *The Elementary Structures of Kinship*—the stated objective is to discern invariant structures or rules behind a mass or tumult of seemingly contradictory ethnographic data. Yet, in *The Savage Mind* we also find the following passage in which Lévi-Strauss seems to re-constitute *la pensée sauvage* as a form of ideology:

> It is of course only for purposes of exposition and because they form the subject of this book that I am apparently giving a sort of priority to ideology and superstructures. I do not at all mean to suggest that ideological transformations give rise to social ones. Only the reverse is in fact true. Men's conception of the relations between nature and culture is a function of modifications of their own social relations. But, since my aim here is to outline a theory of superstructures, reasons of method require that they should be singled out for attention and that major phenomena which have no place in this programme should seem to be left in brackets or given second place. We are however merely studying the shadows on the wall of the Cave without forgetting that it is only the attention we give them which lends them a semblance of reality. (Lévi-Strauss 1966, 117)

It is worth briefly re-stating the fact that Marx' analysis of religion is indebted to that initially developed by Feuerbach. However, in both the *Contribution to The Critique of Hegel's Philosophy of Right* (1844) and the *Theses on Feuerbach* (1845) Marx develops and goes beyond the position set out by Feuerbach, arguing that it is not enough simply to unmask religious truth-claims as false: rather the only way for the illusion of religion to be destroyed is for the destruction of the world that produced it: "the philosophers have only *interpreted* the world, in various ways; the point is to *change* it" (Marx 1992, 423). Religion offers mental compensation for a deficient reality, and a solution to the contradictions of the material world in the realm of imagination and fantasy. Thus, religious consciousness is an inverted attitude precisely because the world or society that produced that consciousness is itself inverted. Religious consciousness is not empty—rather, it has a social basis, namely the inversions or contradictions that lie at the heart of an unjust society. Religion, as the ideological mystification of the real, can only be overcome through the destruction of a world which needs religion in order to exist. A Marxist analysis of religion might then take as its starting point enquiry into those processes through which religious truth-claims are authorized and other claims excluded or marginalized.

It is quite clear from the above that an approach to religion inspired by Marx must take seriously the relationship between symbols and a social formation in order to interrogate notions of power, domination and legitimacy. In *Tristes Tropiques*, Lévi-Strauss engages in a brief discussion of chiefly authority in Nambikwara society, an analysis conducted very much in terms of the Maussian framework of reciprocity that was so essential to the study of kinship. Thus, among the Nambikwara Lévi-Strauss "finds an example of authority that is non-exploitative, based not on a structure of subordination, but on a kind of dynamic equilibrium involving continuous exchange between chief and people, an 'economy' that is the condition of possibility of political consent" (Johnson 2003, 64). However, this analysis begins with the following anecdote, an anecdote that cuts against the grain both of Lévi-Strauss' analysis of chiefly authority among the Nambikwara but also of his analysis of *la pensée sauvage*: two groups of Indians—the Sabané and Tarundé—have merged, but one day, the Sabané chief disappears. He is found later that night naked "and in a most convincing attitude of dejection" (Lévi-Strauss 1992a, 306):

> His [the chief's] account of what had happened was extorted from him by an anxious audience. He explained that he had been carried off by the thunder, which the Nambikwara call *amon* (there had been a storm—heralding the beginning of the rainy season—that same day); the thunder had borne him through the air to a point which he named, twenty-five kilometres away from the encampment (Rio Ananaz), had stripped him of all his adornments, then brought him back in the same way and set him down at the spot where we had found him. The incident was discussed until everybody fell asleep, and the following morning the Sabané chief had recovered not only his usual good humour but also all his adornments too: no one showed any surprise at this, and he offered no explanation. During the next few days, a very different version of the episode began to be repeated among the

Tarundé. They maintained that the chief, under pretence of communicating with the other world, had begun negotiations with the groups of Indians who were camping in the neighbourhood. These insinuations never came to a head, and the official version of the affair was openly accepted. But, in private conversation, the Tarundé chief made no secret of his anxiety. As the two groups left shortly afterwards, I never heard the end of the story.

(Lévi-Strauss 1992a, 306–307)

As Johnson (2003, 66–67) suggests, although Lévi-Strauss stresses that the basis for consent in Nambikwara society is the rule of reciprocity and moreover that the political power of a chief is strictly demarcated off from the spiritual power of a shaman (Lévi-Strauss 1992a, 311), in the anecdote above religion is clearly used by the Sabané chief as a means of dissembling—as the Indians themselves recognize—yet Lévi-Strauss' subsequent analysis is directed entirely towards emptying the office of the chief of any ideological content.

Strangely, in the essay "The Sorcerer and his Magic" we find the same anecdote repeated though this time around it is the shaman and not the chief that disappears, is found and recounts a tale of having been transported away by the thunder (1993h, 169–71). Lévi-Strauss prefaces the story with the following question: "How much credulity and how much scepticism are involved in the attitude of the group toward those in whom it recognizes extraordinary powers, to whom it accords corresponding privileges, but from whom it also requires adequate satisfaction?" (1993h, 169). The answer to this question is posed in terms of social consensus, a shared "gravitational field" (1993h, 168) in this case between the community, the shaman and the patient. Thus, in the story of Quesalid that is also recounted in the essay—the sceptic who becomes a shaman because he does not believe in shamanic techniques of curing yet paradoxically becomes a shaman of great renown—we are told that "Quesalid did not become a great shaman because he cured his patients; he cured his patients because he had become a great shaman" (1993h, 180). It no longer matters that Quesalid and we who read Quesalid's story know that the shamanic techniques in which Quesalid was initiated have no factual basis and actually involve quite deliberate deceit and sleight of hand. Rather, what matters is that the shaman is able to integrate, through performance, the patient's anomalous experience of pain into a meaningful and recognizable totality. Thus, in "The Effectiveness of Symbols" (1993i) in which Lévi-Strauss analyses a Cuna song recited to aid a difficult birth, he claims that what the patient "does not accept are the incoherent and arbitrary pains, which are an alien element in her system but which the shaman, calling upon myth, will re-integrate within a whole where everything is meaningful" (1993i, 197). Just as in the first essay where the efficacy of the shamanic cure is located in the consensus that holds between the community, the shaman and the patient, in the second the effectiveness of the symbols used by the shaman to effect the cure is said to lie in the social structuring and regulating of experience that occurs through participation in a shared language (1993i, 198). Importantly, it does not seem to matter to Lévi-Strauss that the (shamanic) mode through which the patient comes to understand his or her condition is mythical or symbolic or indeed entirely false—"that the mythology of the shaman does not correspond to an objective reality does not matter" (1993i, 197)—according to Lévi-Strauss, all that matters is that the patient, the community and the shaman, together, believe it to be true.

However bones cannot be mended by stories, and nor can tumours be dissolved by simply wishing for it to be so, no matter what public opinion says. As Neu (1975) remarks, Lévi-Strauss surely ought to distinguish between the general consensus of a community regarding the status of a shaman in relation to the shaman's actual ability to heal the sick (Neu 1975, 287). Yet, Lévi-Strauss argues that shamanic symbolism is effective not only because it provides the patient and the community with a language with which to organize and draw meaning from disturbing events and experiences but also because that mythico-symbolic language actually corresponds or accords with a deeper reality. As such, in "The Effectiveness of Symbols" Lévi-Strauss argues for a parallel between the shaman and the psychoanalyst, between the theories of each and physiological theory (1993i, 198–204). Thus, beneath the Cuna song that is to be recited in instances of difficult birth lies the truth of a physiological reality—the myth does not simply recount a "mythical itinerary" and describe a mythical realm, but symbolically represents the "vagina and uterus of the pregnant woman" (1993i, 188). According to Lévi-Strauss, then, shamanism and psychoanalysis are parallel to the extent that each refers, metaphorically, to physiology:

> Given this hypothesis…the shamanistic cure and the psychoanalytic cure would become strictly parallel. It would be a matter, either way, of stimulating an organic transformation which would consist essentially in a structural reorganization, by inducing the patient intensively to live out a myth—either received or created by him—whose structure would be, at the unconscious level, analogous to the structure whose genesis is sought on the organic level. The effectiveness of symbols would consist precisely in this "inductive property," by which formally homologous structures, built out of different materials at different levels of life—organic processes, unconscious mind, rational thought—are related to one another. Poetic metaphor provides a familiar example of this inductive process, but as a rule it does not tran-

scend the unconscious level. Thus we note the significance of Rimbaud's intuition that metaphor can change the world.

(Lévi-Strauss 1993i, 201–02)

We are asked to accept, then, that the shaman's symbols and myths, like those of the psychoanalyst, can actually induce physiological changes and cures though it is never explained how or why this should be the case. Indeed, in both essays Lévi-Strauss deploys the psychoanalytic notion "abreaction" (1993h, 181; 1993i, 198) to conceptualize the means by which the shaman induces the patient to live out the myth. But in psychoanalysis abreaction refers to the moment when, during psychoanalytic treatment, the patient relives and as it were "discharges" the situation which lies at the root of his or her disturbance. The difficulty here is that in psychoanalysis it is the patient that "abreacts" whereas in shamanism it is the shaman (Neu 1975, 290). It seems doubtful, then, whether the parallel that Lévi-Strauss seeks to draw between shamanism and psychoanalysis is in any sense productive and, moreover, whether the theories of each really parallel physiology and even if the latter was true, whether that fact would actually explain anything (Neu 1975, 291).

Lévi-Strauss' discussion of chiefly power, shamanism and symbolism clearly provides a point of departure to ask questions about the social processes through consensus is produced and regulated, about the codification of authority and the authentication of political and religious or magical power, about the social and historical processes of group formation and identification, about how symbolic meanings are authorized by interpretive communities and other possible meanings excluded, and about the production and codification of experience and of the body through, in this case, shamanic ritual practice and discourse (Asad 1983, 251). These are precisely the kinds of questions we might expect an anthropologist inspired by the substantive aspects of Marx' writings, to ask. As such, we are beginning to become aware of some of the shortcomings of Lévi-Strauss' structural anthropology: it seems incapable of asking questions that are properly socio-logical.

Ideology and material culture

In *Tristes Tropiques* (1992a) Lévi-Strauss engages in an analysis of Caduveo art, particularly the body painting done by the women of the tribe. We are told that Caduveo society is organized into three endogamous castes, and the style or type of body decoration is related to the caste-group to which the body belongs. According to Lévi-Strauss, the fact of endogamous castes and the rankings internal to the caste groups, means that it is increasingly difficult for marriages to conform to the necessities of the status system—as such, there is a contradiction between the biological reproduction of the social group as a whole and the social reproduction of hierarchy. Whereas other tribal groups organized along similar lines have overcome this contradiction by further division into exogamous moieties such that "the asymmetry of the classes was...counterbalanced by the symmetry of the moieties" (1992a, 196), this is not the case for the Caduveo:

> They therefore never had the opportunity of resolving their contradictions or at least of concealing them by means of artful institutions. But the remedy they failed to use on the social level, or which they refused to consider, could not elude them completely; it continued to haunt them in an insidious way. And since they could not become conscious of it and live it out in reality, they began to dream about it. Not in a direct form, which would have clashed with their prejudices, but in a transposed, and seemingly innocuous, form: in their art. If my analysis is correct, in the last resort the graphic art of the Caduveo women is to be interpreted, and its mysterious appeal and seemingly gratuitous complexity to be explained, as the phantasm of a society ardently and insatiably seeking a means of expressing symbolically the institutions it might have, if its interests and superstitions did not stand in the way. (Lévi-Strauss 1992a, 196–97)

Art, then, among the Caduveo, constitutes a realm in which contradictions which cannot be solved at the material level of society can be posed and overcome. Here, Lévi-Strauss acknowledges a strong relationship between a mode of social organization and an ideational realm. The difference between the mode of interpretation adopted here and the more recognizably structuralist model used for the interpretation of myth is surely striking.

Summary

In this chapter I have attempted to do two things: first to link Lévi-Strauss' analyses of totemism and myth to his general concept of *la pensée sauvage* and his assault on evolutionist theories of magic and religion and, secondly, to cover some essays and anecdotes in which the analysis is somewhat at odds with the structuralist approach and which as such opens Lévi-Strauss to a number of possible critiques. Highlighting such inconsistencies is not part of a strategy to undermine or dismiss Lévi-Strauss' contribution to anthropology and the study of religions. Rather, it demonstrates the breadth of Lévi-Strauss' *oeuvre* and the importance of a sustained and detailed reading of that *oeuvre* in order to bring out the subtleties and nuances of the work.

Chapter 6

The structure of nostalgia

> I wish I had lived in the days of *real* journeys, when it was still possible to see the full splendour of a spectacle that had not yet been blighted, polluted and spoilt; I wished I had not trodden the ground as myself, but as Bernier, Tavernier or Manucci did...Once embarked upon this guessing game can continue indefinitely. When was the best time to see India? At what period would the study of Brazilian savages have afforded the purest satisfaction, and revealed them in their least adulterated state? Would it have been better to arrive in Rio in the eighteenth century with Bougainville, or in the sixteenth with Léry and Thevet? For every five years I move back in time, I am able to save a custom, gain a ceremony or share in another belief. But I know the texts too well not to realize that, by going back a century, I am at the same time forgoing data and lines of enquiry which would offer intellectual enrichment. And so I am caught within a circle from which there is no escape: the less human societies were able to communicate with each other and therefore to corrupt each other through contact, the less their respective emissaries were able to perceive the wealth and significance of their diversity. In short, I have only two possibilities: either I can be like some traveller of the olden days, who was faced with a stupendous spectacle, all, or almost all, of which eluded him, or worse still, filled him with scorn and disgust; or I can be a modern traveller, chasing after the vestiges of a vanished reality. I lose on both counts, and more seriously than at first may appear, for, while I complain of being able to glimpse no more than the shadow of the past, I may be insensitive to reality as it is taking shape at this very moment, since I have not reached the stage of development at which I would be capable of perceiving it. A few hundred years hence, in this same place, another traveller, as despairing as myself, will mourn the disappearance of what I might have seen, but failed to see. I am subject to a double infirmity: all that I perceive offends me, and I constantly reproach myself for not seeing as much as I should.
>
> (Lévi-Strauss, *Tristes Tropiques*)

So far, our critical exposition of Lévi-Strauss' writings has been focused squarely on his contributions to the anthropology of kinship, totemism, myth, shamanism and the thought and material culture of so-called primitive societies. However, beyond the narrow corpus of what Lévi-Strauss

---

In this chapter:

- Introduction to Lévi-Strauss' 'political' writings and his critique of 'the West' in *Tristes Tropiques*.

- Introduction to Lévi-Strauss' discussion of writing and Jacques Derrida's critique.

- Discussion of Lévi-Strauss' distinction between 'hot' and 'cold' societies.

- Discussion and analysis of Lévi-Strauss' critiques of globalization, 'mono-culture,' and Jean-Paul Sartre's notion of history as progress and humanism.

- Discussion and analysis of Lévi-Strauss' views on Buddhism and Islam.

---

himself might describe as "scientific" works, lies a body of writings that deals with other political and philosophical questions and problems. As such, we should understand Lévi-Strauss' anthropology as incorporating a generalized critique of (Western) values that follows a distinctive tradition of French writers from Montaigne, Montesquieu, Diderot, Rousseau, Gide and Camus (Steiner 1970, 172). As Tilley notes, this other Lévi-Strauss has written significant and powerful critiques of "the mass culture of the 'civilized' West, the effects of colonization and global capitalist expansion, ethnocentrism and social evolutionary schemes, racism, notions of progress and technological development, and associated environmental destruction" (Tilley 1990, 48). In this chapter, then, we will seek to situate Lévi-Strauss' structural anthropology within wider debates about globalization and minority peoples, racism and the idea of progress, humanism and the environment and religion, holding in mind the fact that these writings were composed in a historical period of great upheaval and turmoil that witnessed the defeat of Nazism in Western Europe and the "de-colonization" of Africa and Asia.

The structure of nostalgia

Tristes Tropiques is a beautiful book. All the critics have said as much. Yet, given Lévi-Strauss' repeated insistence that cultural products arise not from the subjective intentions of individual authors but are rather constituted in advance by some deep and distant, organizing and essentially a-temporal grammar, it is a strange book. We surely could not have anticipated a committed structuralist to have written a highly autobiographical account of his field work expeditions in South America, though we should at all times be aware of the extent to which this account has been edited to create a sense of the solitary anthropologist grappling with the apparent strangeness of his objects of study and, moreover, that it entirely omits the period he spent in New York during the war years and his meeting with Roman Jakobson (Johnson 2003, 173–74). Moreover, given the highly technical focus of his anthropological writings and the frequent appeals to a discourse of scientific neutrality, detachment and objectivity, we could not have predicted just how profoundly subjective and political this book is. Indeed, given the apparently cold and aloof tenor of his anthropological writings, we further could not have expected the extent to which *Tristes Tropiques* is structured by emotionally charged tropes of tragedy, loss and nostalgia:

> Journeys, those magic caskets full of dreamlike promises, will never again yield up their treasures untarnished. A proliferating and overexcited civilization has broken the silence of the seas once and for all. The perfumes of the tropics and pristine freshness of human beings have been corrupted by a busyness with dubious implications, which mortifies our desires and dooms us to acquire only contaminated memories.
>
> (Lévi-Strauss 1992a, 38)

Furthermore, this profound sense of nostalgia is combined, in no uncertain terms, with a critique of "the West" and the violence it has visited upon the unsuspecting inhabitants of the forests of Brazil and elsewhere:

> Now that the Polynesian islands have been smothered in concrete and turned into aircraft carriers solidly anchored in the southern seas, when the whole of Asia is beginning to look like a dingy suburb, when shantytowns are spreading across Africa, when civil and military aircraft blight the primeval innocence of the American or Melanesian forests even before destroying their virginity, what else can the so-called escapism of travelling do than confront us with the more unfortunate aspects of our history? Our great Western civilization, which has created the marvels we now enjoy, has only succeeded in producing them at the cost of corresponding ills. The order and harmony of the Western world, its most famous achievement, and a laboratory in which structures of a complexity as yet unknown are being fashioned, demand the elimination of a prodigious mass of noxious by-products which now contaminate the globe. The first thing we see as we travel round the world is our own filth, thrown into the face of mankind.
>
> (Lévi-Strauss 1992a, 38)

Through a brilliant deconstructive reading of *Tristes Tropiques*, Derrida demonstrates the extent to which what he calls "the metaphysics of presence" structures Lévi-Strauss' critique of "the West" and impassioned defence of minority peoples. In two chapters titled "On the Line" and

"A Writing Lesson," Lévi-Strauss recounts an incident that took place during his field work with the Nambikwara in Brazil. His work among them had been complicated from the start by the fact that the Nambikwara are forbidden from using proper names. When one day he was playing with some children, one little girl hit another. The victim approached the anthropologist and whispered a secret in his ear, but Lévi-Strauss could not understand what she was saying. The perpetrator saw what was happening and tried to tell him a second secret. "After some hesitation and questioning," writes Lévi-Strauss, "the meaning of the incident became clear. Out of revenge, the first little girl had come to tell me the name of her enemy, and the latter, on becoming aware of this, had retaliated by confiding to me the other's name" (Lévi-Strauss 1992a, 279). The "lesson" Lévi-Strauss draws from this episode is the corruption of authentic sociality by the introduction of writing—the violence of naming interrupts and disturbs the pure presence of the primitive community and is, moreover, introduced from the outside by the foreigner, Lévi-Strauss himself. "This incapacity [for writing]," Derrida suggests, "will be presently thought, within the ethico-political order, as an innocence and a non-violence interrupted by the forced entry of the West" (1997, 110). As such, Derrida draws our attention to Lévi-Strauss' romantic representation of the Nambikwara as "among the most primitive to be found anywhere in the world" (1992a, 272) and as "survivors from the Stone Age" (1992a, 276):

> On the dark savannah, the camp fires sparkle. Near their warmth, which offers the only protection against the growing chill of the night; behind the frail screens of palm-fronds and branches, hurriedly set up on the side from which rain and wind are expected; next to the baskets filled with the pathetic possessions which constitute the community's earthly wealth; lying on the bare ground which stretches away in all directions and is haunted by other equally hostile and apprehensive bands, husbands and wives, closely intertwined, are aware of being each other's support and comfort, and the only help against day-to-day difficulties and that brooding melancholy which settles from time to time on the souls of the Nambikwara. The visitor camping with the Indians in the bush for the first time, is filled with anguish and pity at the sight of human beings so totally bereft; some relentless cataclysm seems to have crushed them against the ground in a hostile land, leaving them naked and shivering by their flickering fires. He gropes his way through the scrub, taking care not to knock against the hands, arms or chests that he glimpses as warm reflections in the glow of the flames. But the wretchedness is shot through with whisperings and chuckles. The couples embrace as if seeking to recapture a lost unity, and their caresses continue uninterrupted as he goes by. He can sense in all of them an immense kindness, a profoundly carefree attitude, a naive and charming animal satisfaction—and binding these various feelings together—something which might be called

the most truthful and moving expression of human love.
(Lévi-Strauss 1992a, 293)

In this condition of innocence and of pure presence, Lévi-Strauss draws out the lesson of writing from among the Nambikwara—a people without writing. Writing, claims Lévi-Strauss, has a "sociological rather than an intellectual purpose" (1992a, 298). Indeed, elsewhere, Lévi-Strauss claims that the advent of writing has deprived us of "something fundamental" (1993f, 366):

> It is, rather, modern societies that should be defined in negative terms. Our relations with one another are now only occasionally and fragmentarily based upon global experience, the concrete "apprehension" of one person by another. They are largely the result of a process of indirect reconstruction, through written documents. We are no longer linked to our past by an oral tradition which implies direct contact with others (storytellers, priests, wise men, or elders), but by books amassed in libraries, books from which we endeavour—with extreme difficulty—to form a picture of their authors. And we communicate with the immense majority of our contemporaries by all kinds of intermediaries—written documents or administrative machinery—which undoubtedly vastly extend our contacts but at the same time make those contacts somewhat "inauthentic." (Lévi-Strauss 1993f, 366)

As such, Lévi-Strauss suggests that the invention or advent of writing cannot be used as a measure to distinguish between so-called savage and civilized peoples, the former without history or a past except in terms of that which remains within the recall of a living individual, the latter able to account for their past achievements through the archive and the library and as such "progress." Rather Lévi-Strauss, in anarchistic fashion, links writing to the advent of violence, the political and the state:

> The only phenomenon with which writing has always been concomitant is the creation of cities and empires, that is the integration of large numbers of individuals into a political system, and their grading into castes or classes... it seems to have favoured the exploitation of human beings rather than their enlightenment...My hypothesis, if correct, would oblige us to recognize the fact that the primary function of written communication is to facilitate slavery. (Lévi-Strauss 1992a, 299)

Derrida directs his critical attention to the violence that supposedly precipitated the whole incident and the "ethnocentrism" that Lévi-Strauss is consciously writing against but yet, according to Derrida, is simultaneously reproducing:

> Only an innocent community...only a micro-society of non-violence and freedom, all the members of which can by rights remain within range of an immediate and transparent, a "crystalline" address, fully self-present in its living speech, only such a community can suffer, as the surprise of an

aggression coming *from without*, the insinuation of writing, the infiltration of its "ruse" and of its "perfidy." Only such a community can import *from abroad* "the exploitation of man by man." (Derrida 1997, 119)

The violence of naming occasioned by the outsider Lévi-Strauss is analogous to the violence of writing which is likewise held to be outside or exterior to speech. However, according to Derrida this violence that seems to have accidentally befallen the community and speech from the outside is inscribed in language from the very beginning. According to Derrida, language is a system of relations and differences—language is characterized by the "play" of signifiers which point not to any stable ground beyond or outside language but only to other signifiers. Signifiers differentiate and defer such that no thing—neither consciousness nor world—can ever be purely present because they are always mediated by the (violence) of signs. As such, Lévi-Strauss' "logo-centrism" and the conceptualization of writing as violence only reproduces the dominant terms and categories through which the West has privileged speech and presence as the authentic grounds of meaning and truth.

Derrida's critique is exquisite but also perhaps misappropriates the strategic essentialism that is central both to Lévi-Strauss' critique of "the West" and his defence of minority peoples. The picture painted by Lévi-Strauss of the Nambikwara is designed to evoke not merely sympathy, but an empathic connection to the plight of other human beings who, through no fault of their own, have been decimated by disease and whose societies and cultures are on the verge of extinction, conditions directly attributable to the expansion of Western techniques of agriculture, industry, urbanism and the expansion of capitalism to the most remote parts of the world. Lévi-Strauss is well aware that the global hegemony of the West rests ultimately not on consent but force, and he suggests that this fact "is an objective phenomenon which can only be explained by calling upon objective causes" (1994a, 346). However, no such explication of "objective causes" is offered, though *Tristes Tropiques* does contain suggestions for the points of departure such an analysis might take (see also Lévi-Strauss 1994g, 312–16). However, even as the reader is being drawn into to an appreciation of the scale of the threat to these different kinds of human life, Lévi-Strauss is simultaneously, as Pace notes, describing the Nambikwara as a "laboratory for social anthropology" and that "the particular interest offered us by the Nambikwara is that they confront us with one of the simplest forms of social and political organization" (Pace 1986, 16). On the one hand, then, the Nambikwara are co-subjects linked to us in a relation of empathy that demands that we reflexively change those globalized structures that threaten their existence while on the other, they are objects of a scientific curiosity precisely because of the poverty of their technical expertise that elsewhere, Lévi-Strauss argues, is a completely spurious and indeed ethnocentric manner of relating to another culture.

Derrida's critique also misses the point that Lévi-Strauss' linking of speech and writing with specific kinds of fraternity could open up some important questions as to the articulation of modes of communication and exchange with modes of social organization. For example, Anderson's claim that print media provided new ways for imagining sociality and indeed stands in a determining relationship if we want to understand the emergence of nations and nationalism (Anderson 1991, 36) or, given Lévi-Strauss' fascination for computers, McLuhan's claim that the advent of new forms of mediation such as digital media coincides with or indeed causes the emergence of new forms of sociality that transcend local and national boundaries that necessitates the investigation of the processes through which locality is constituted in a globalizing world (Appadurai 1996, 52; Gupta and Ferguson 2001, 4) are outstanding examples of this kind of questioning. Indeed, McLuhan's assertion that "the medium is the message" (2004, 7) is precisely intended to draw attention to the fact that "the 'message' of any medium or technology is the change of scale or pace or pattern that it introduces into human affairs" (2004, 8). Mass media, according to both McLuhan and Anderson, fill the void created by the evacuation of religion from public society. Mass media provide the fraternal bonds and linkages that will bind individuals to one another, although the thrust of critical theory such as that of the Frankfurt School assumes that mass media are in fact incapable of generating authentic or meaningful sociality. Lévi-Strauss, however, does not interrogate these processes, content to inscribe a rather crude series of oppositions between "primitive" and "modern" societies where the former are associated with speech and *la pensée sauvage* and are characterized as "cold" but also as egalitarian and stable while the latter are associated with writing, science and are characterized as "hot," hierarchical and are therefore unstable. Moreover, Lévi-Strauss also suggests that so-called cold societies "have developed...a particular wisdom which impels them to resist...any modification in their structure that would enable history to burst into their midst" (Lévi-Strauss 1994d, 28; see also Lévi-Strauss 1994g, 319–20).

The pivotal concept in these distinctions is entropy: the second law of thermodynamics states that isolated systems tend towards disorder or "thermic death." This movement from order to disorder is irreversible unless or until the system opens itself up to exchange with what was previously outside the system. If entropy is to be understood as energy, then the law states that no system can survive on energy drawn only from itself or its own resources—it must find alternative sources of energy from beyond its boundaries (Bauman 1999, 47) (This image of an isolated system opening itself up to exchange is not merely the arrest of entropy or even entry into a network, but also another mode of envisioning Lévi-Strauss' argument about exogamy as the overcoming of incest [see chapter two]). As such, according to Lévi-Strauss, so-called cold societies are akin to clocks. The social environment is highly structured, and though there is, in these societies, a low level of technological sophistication, there is on the other hand a high level of cohesion and stability. So-called hot societies, by contrast, are akin to steam engines and the by-product of such a machine is a high-level of entropy or disorder. These distinctions resemble rather closely Durkheim's distinction between "mechanical" and "organic" forms of social solidarity, but unlike Durkheim Lévi-Strauss makes no attempt to analyse the social processes through which fraternal linkages and articulations are fabricated and sustained in these different kinds of society (Johnson 2003, 122). Once again, the highly abstract and formal style of structuralist analysis actually appears to prevent any satisfactory account of global processes refracted at the national and local levels which simultaneously facilitate the "heroic" explorations of anthropologists and the liquidation of cultural diversity. If, as Lévi-Strauss suggests, the global expansion of Western modernity has led to ethnocide, then surely it is incumbent on Lévi-Strauss to actually explicate and theorize how and why this should be the case, and moreover to provide us with some kind of alternative political vision.

Furthermore, we might ask ourselves to what extent Lévi-Strauss' romanticization of the Nambikwara, of face-to-face relations and of speech and authenticity is not entirely at odds with the broad thrust of a structuralist anthropology that depends and is exemplary of the very violence which Lévi-Strauss so passionately condemns and which takes as its object of study the anthropological canon seeking to re-construct not any local or indigenous point of view but rather unconscious structures and structuring processes behind local systems of classification or totemism and mythological accounts of the origins of fire, tobacco and wild pigs (among others). Surely the reduction of cultural differences to different permutations of a single binary opposition and the claim that myths and classificatory systems from different times and places are all examples of a single logic is an element of those wider, global processes of standardization and homogenization that Lévi-Strauss is seeking to oppose.

Lévi-Strauss' passionate and indeed engaged defence of the world's disappearing cultural minorities is a worthy legacy, but how far does he recognize and acknowledge his own complicity in the very process-es of globalization he is writing against? Lévi-Strauss argues in *Tristes Tropiques* that "mankind has opted for monoculture" (1992a, 38), a phrase that seems reminiscent of the fears articulated by the likes of Adorno and Horkheimer and Marcuse in their respective critiques of mass society and the flattening out and standardization of culture they attributed to the advance of capitalism and processes of commodification (Adorno and Horkheimer 1944, 120; Marcuse 1964, 31). Lévi-Strauss' critique of so-called "mono-culture" is developed most fully in the essays "Race and History" (1994a) and "Race and Culture" (1985e) and is framed in terms that function to elide any overt political content. It is to these essays that we now must turn.

Diversity and extinction

We have already noted, *vis-à-vis* Lévi-Strauss' approach to myth, the extent to which that approach functioned to disarticulate myths as poten-tial ideological vehicles from any social context and to transpose them to a scientific realm where, we might assume, they can be rendered harmless and docile objects of structural analysis. Lévi-Strauss' defence of minori-ties, his critique of racism and ethnocentrism and his argument for cultural diversity though obviously political, is nevertheless similarly conducted in terms of a natural science discourse of adaptations, mutations, demo-graphics and genetics the result of which shifts the grounds of the argu-ment towards highly abstract terrain. In "Race and History" Lévi-Strauss argues that the evolutionist hypothesis—an hypothesis which seeks to account for cultural differences in terms of technological development—actually annuls difference by transforming non-Western cultures into stag-es of the West's own distant past (1994a, 330–35). As Lévi-Strauss points out, just because "their history is…unknown" does not mean "that it does not exist" (1994a, 335). Indeed, we are conditioned to interpret and under-stand cultural differences in a particular way:

> We would…see as cumulative any culture which developed in a way analo-gous to ours—in other words, whose development would have a *meaning* for us. Whereas the other cultures would seem to us static—not neces-sarily because they are so, but because their line of development means nothing to us and cannot be measured in terms of the system of references we use. (Lévi-Strauss 1994a, 339)

In other words, in order to understand other cultures we must embrace a complete change of perspective. As such, Lévi-Strauss suggests that anthropology provides an appropriate standpoint from which to understand other cultures, as anthropology provides the necessary tools from which to understand other systems of thought from the inside and from without. Indeed, this is precisely the ground of Lévi-Strauss' critique of Jean-Paul Sartre in the final chapter of *The Savage Mind*. Sartre's view of history as unitary and the linked assumption that it is only the societies of the West that have achieved historical self-consciousness leads Lévi-Strauss to accuse Sartre of ethnocentrism and of being incapable of relating to other cultures except in terms of the categories of his own culture. Moreover, Lévi-Strauss also pointedly re-writes the founding event of the French Revolution—the origin of the West's self-consciousness of itself as historical—as myth (Johnson 2003, 127–30).

In opposition to Sartre's unitary, cumulative or incremental view of history in which time is understood as progress, Lévi-Strauss argues that history proceeds rather in "leaps and bounds, or as the biologists would say, by mutations" (1994a, 337). He introduces the notion of chance via the image of the gambler whose moves and choices depend on each successive throw of the dice. This re-formulation of history away from reason's contemplation of itself manifest in some enigmatic and hidden *telos* towards a notion of history as radical contingency allows Lévi-Strauss to suggest that cumulative history is not the preserve of certain cultures over certain others but rather the product of luck and most significantly, interaction or "coalition" with other cultures (1994a, 356).

In "Race and Culture," Lévi-Strauss continues the argument though it is formulated in explicitly genetic terms:

> Over thirty years ago…I used the notion of coalition to explain that isolated cultures cannot hope to create by themselves the conditions for a truly cumulative history. For such conditions, I said, diverse cultures must voluntarily or involuntarily combine their respective stakes, thereby giving themselves a better chance to realize, in the great game of history, the long winning series that allows history to progress. Geneticists now express similar views on biological evolution…in the history of populations, genetic recombination plays a part comparable to that of cultural recombination in the evolution of the ways of life, the techniques, the bodies of knowledge, and the beliefs whose distribution distinguishes the various societies.
>
> (Lévi-Strauss 1985e, 17–18)

Johnson (2003, 115) suggests that the homology drawn by Lévi-Strauss between cultural and biological change or adaptation means that he is proposing a stochastic model of historical change. We might assume that one outcome of such a line of argument—for cultural diversity and against globalizing mono-culture; against the view that non-Western cultures and societies are in any sense backward or inferior to Western cultures and societies; against history-as-progress and instead for time as discontinuous and subject to random and unpredictable outcomes—would be to argue for the preservation of minority cultures against the pernicious violence of capitalist expansion and globalization. Yet, this is not what Lévi-Strauss suggests at all. Indeed, what Lévi-Strauss argues for sounds rather reminiscent of Tylor who, in the closing lines of *Primitive Culture* (1903) declared anthropology to be "a reformer's science" whose task would be to "expose the remains of crude old culture which have passed into harmful superstition, and to mark these out for destruction" (1903, 453):

> The necessity of preserving the diversity of cultures, in a world threatened by monotony and uniformity, has certainly not remained unnoticed by international institutions. They must also understand that, to reach this goal, it will not be enough to favour local traditions and to allow some respite to times gone by. It is the fact of diversity which must be saved, not the historical content given to it by each era (and which no era could perpetuate beyond itself). We must listen to the wheat growing, encourage secret potentialities, awaken all the vocations to live together that history holds in reserve. One must also be ready to consider without surprise, repulsion, or revolt whatever unusual aspect all these new social forms of expression cannot fail to present. Tolerance is not a contemplative position, dispensing indulgence to what was and to what is. It is a dynamic attitude consisting in the foresight, the understanding, and the promotion of what wants to be. The diversity of human cultures is behind us, and ahead of us. The only demand we may make upon it…is that it realize itself in forms such that each is a contribution to the greater generosity of the others.
>
> (Lévi-Strauss 1994a, 362)

Lévi-Strauss suggests that although cultural diversity is preferable to mono-culture, the blanket preservation of different beliefs and practices is not the solution. Indeed, those diversities which are the residues of previous collaborations between cultures may constitute "putrefied vestiges" that threaten the overall health of the "international body" and which therefore "must be pruned, amputated, if need be, to facilitate the birth of other forms of adaptation" (1994a, 361). Nowhere does Lévi-Strauss indicate how decisions about the health or sickness of the global body would be made or on what criteria, except that they would be the preserve of "international institutions" (1994a, 361). However, elsewhere Lévi-Strauss does indicate that at the heart of anthropology lies a sense of "compassion" (Lévi-Strauss 1994b, 38) as if the anthropologists, as the conscience of the West, might be best qualified to have their knowledge and professional and scientific beneficence deployed in the interests of some higher purpose and to decide which cultural practices are vital and which are redundant. This, however, is surely the politics of the glass bead game.

Structuralism, humanism and ecology

It has been said that structuralism is an anti-humanism. Certainly Lévi-Strauss' critique of phenomenology and existentialism (see chapter one) express a profound dissatisfaction with ways of thinking and theorizing that he feels reify the individual subject. In this sense, structuralism is against humanism to the extent that humanism assumes the individual human subject to be the privileged object of philosophical reflection and a self-evident ground for the knowledge generated through such reflection. However, I think it would be incorrect to say that Lévi-Strauss wants to do away with the subject: rather he wants to modify it such that it takes on an ecological dimension wherein subject-hood is extended not only to all human beings but indeed to all the entities that share life on our planet (see Lévi-Strauss 1985f, 282). Lévi-Strauss finds a precedent for this point of view among so-called primitive peoples whom he claims display "a deep respect for...nature" (1994g, 319). Lévi-Strauss notes that all societies make a distinction between nature and culture but it is only in the West that nature is seen as being entirely subservient to culture. A positive value is thus implicitly attributed by Lévi-Strauss to that mode of thought, that "logic of the concrete," discussed in *Totemism* and *The Savage Mind*. On the other hand, he claims that "respect for life...does not exist in a society determined to destroy irreplaceable forms of life, whether animal or vegetable" (1994c, 285) in the name of scientific and technical progress. As such,

> A well-ordered humanism does not begin with itself. By setting mankind apart from the rest of creation, Western humanism has deprived it of a safeguard. The moment man knows no limit to his power, he sets about destroying himself. Look at the death camps and, on another level, with its insidious effects but equally tragic consequences for all of humanity, pollution. (Lévi-Strauss and Eribon 1991, 162)

What then, is the solution? After all, as we have seen throughout this chapter, Lévi-Strauss eschews either a properly socio-historical analysis of issues such as colonialism, racism or globalization, while his critique of humanism—however well-intentioned—could actually imperil the efforts of human rights activists to defend the rights of minorities against states and multi-national corporations. Towards the end of *Tristes Tropiques*, Lévi-Strauss suggests that the value of (structural) anthropology lies in its representation or modelling of other modes of sociality that could be applied for the reform of our own society and "to elucidate principles of social life that we can apply in reforming our own customs" (Lévi-Strauss 1992a, 392). Elsewhere, he has suggested that a new humanism would necessitate that we

Found the rights of man not, as we have done since the American and French Revolutions, on the unique and privileged character of one living species, but instead to see it as a special case of the rights of all species. By moving in that direction…we would be in a position to obtain a larger consensus than is possible when we confine ourselves solely to the rights of man, since this view has historical links with Stoic philosophy and, at a distance, with the philosophies of the Orient. We would even find ourselves on an equal footing with the practical attitude that "primitive" peoples, the ones studied by anthropologists, have regarding nature. They sometimes lack an explicit theory, but the precepts they observe have the same consequences. (Lévi-Strauss and Eribon 1991, 163)

Lévi-Strauss' social theory, in the last analysis, amounts to a commitment to the idea that we will only re-enchant the world if we are willing to listen to the wisdom of those peoples who we have pushed to the brink of destruction. Yet, paradoxically it is a social theory that entirely neglects to analyse those socio-historical processes that Lévi-Strauss claims to be writing against.

Nostalgia and religion

Lévi-Strauss formulated the conjunction of structural linguistics and social anthropology very much in terms of an aloof and disinterested concern for science and knowledge as a search for rules: for example, rules of marriage, the logic of local taxonomies and systems of classification and the structural transformations of myth. Even where Lévi-Strauss has ventured, as it were, outside the high walls of the University to intervene in debates with explicit political content he has always sought to conduct that intervention on non-political terrain and to shift the debate away from any potentially agonistic realm towards the Stoicism of the academy. This stoicism and structuralism as a philosophy without a subject might explain Lévi-Strauss' interest in Buddhism which, in *Tristes Tropiques*, he describes as enshrining "universal kindliness" (1992a, 403). It must be said that Lévi-Strauss displays little or no interest in or knowledge of the intricacies of Buddhist philosophy or, for that matter, of the fact of political Buddhism and the implication of the *sangha* in countries such as Thailand with the formation of nationalist ideologies, programmes of centralization and modernization and the neutralization of dissent (Jackson 2002, 155–88; Keyes 1989, 139–41; Sukatipan 1995, 193–223). We might interpret this as an instance of reverse Orientalism (Clarke 1997; King 1999; Said 1995) in the manner of Mircea Eliade, Herman Hesse or Jack Kerouac in which some aspect of the Orient or the East is singled out as a source for the potential and beneficial re-enchantment of the West.

Interestingly, Lévi-Strauss' remarks about Buddhism are juxtaposed with equally ill-informed comments about Islam which is constructed as Buddhism's opposite. As such,

> Symbolic of Moslem culture...[is the accumulation of] the most subtle refinements—palaces made of precious stones, fountains of rose-water, dishes of food coated with gold leaf and tobacco mixed with pounding pearls—and uses them as a veneer to conceal rustic customs and the bigotry permeating Islamic moral and religious thought...This great religion [Islam] is based not so much on revealed truth as on an inability to establish links with the outside world...Moslem intolerance takes an unconscious form among those who are guilty of it; although they do not always seek to make others share their truth by brutal coercion, they are nevertheless (and this is more serious) incapable of tolerating the existence of others as others. (Lévi-Strauss 1992a, 401–403)

Given the manner of Lévi-Strauss' critique of evolutionist anthropology and of the thinking of Sartre for their respective failure, in his eyes, to relate to so-called primitive societies except in terms of categories and terms imbued with ethnocentrism, racism and the feeling of superiority that the so-called white man's burdened conferred, these are surely extraordinary remarks. This unremittingly negative representation of Islam and of Islamic cultures dismisses at a stroke the diversity of belief and practice within Islam and the variety and complexity of Islamic histories and cultures from Africa, the Middle East, South and central Asia to China and Southeast Asia. Given the authority that has been bestowed on the voice emanating from the hallowed halls of the French academy, to make pronouncements that are surely entirely based in prejudice rather than fact is to betray the very academic ideals Lévi-Strauss has spent his entire life attempting to honour.

Summary

In this chapter I have focused on Lévi-Strauss' political writings. Although I have been highly critical of Lévi-Strauss the public intellectual, I find myself in broad sympathy both with the conscientiousness with which Lévi-Strauss pursued his analyses of kinship, "totemism" and myth and with the political interventions on behalf of minority peoples, his attacks on ethnocentrism and racism and his attempt to reformulate humanism to encompass more than just humankind. However, his inability to theorize the historical structures that actually produce and sustain phenomena such as poverty and inequality is surely a serious failing.

Chapter 7

Lévi-Strauss and the study of religions

As a teenager I was very intolerant on the subject [of religion]. Today, after studying and teaching the history of religions—all kinds of religions—I am more respectful than I was at eighteen or twenty. And besides, even if I remain deaf to religious answers, I am more and more penetrated by the feeling that the cosmos, and man's place in the universe, surpasses and always will surpass our understanding. It happens that I get along better with believers than with out-and-out rationalists. At least the first have a sense of mystery—a mystery that the mind, it seems to me, is inherently incapable of solving. One has to be satisfied with the fact that scientific knowledge nibbles tirelessly away at its edges. But I know of nothing more stimulating or enriching than to try to follow this knowledge as a layman, being all the while aware that every advance raises new problems and that the task is unending.

(Claude Lévi-Strauss, *Conversations with Claude Lévi-Strauss*)

Johnson (2003, 185) suggests that there is an "*excess* of cohesion" across Lévi-Strauss' writings. Pace (1986, 10), by contrast, argues that Lévi-Strauss' works can be separated into "a neo-positivist strain" and a second "humanistically oriented" corpus. In this book I have assumed the latter: we have dealt with Lévi-Strauss' anthropological writings and political writings in separate chapters to bring out the contradictions between the "scientific" writings composed for a narrow audience of specialists on the one hand and, on the other, the writings with a strong political content aimed beyond a specialist, academic readership. In this, the final chapter of this book, we will engage in a strategic juxtaposition of Lévi-Strauss'

In this chapter:

- Discussion of recent theoretical debates in the study of religions.
- Juxtaposition of the phenomenology of religion and structuralism.

---

approach to religions and that of phenomenology. We will take this tack because the phenomenology of religion has been the dominant theoretical and methodological approach to the study of religions in the West for some time: as such, positioning structuralism and phenomenology side by side might provide some interesting points of departure regarding the shape and contour of current theoretical and methodological debates in the study of religions.

In the Preface I offered a brief outline of the phenomenology of religion paying particular attention to three key methodological concepts: first, the idea that religion is a phenomenon *sui generis*, secondly that as such it must be encountered as it is and without prejudice (*epoché*) and thirdly, that the interiority of the believer's commitment must be accessed empathetically. This summary is hardly contentious and need not detain us further. However, what is important to note is the fact that debates about theory and method in the study of religions have typically been conducted in terms of Wilhelm Dilthey's classical methodological opposition of the *naturwissenschaften* to the *geisteswissenschaften*—of the so-called natural sciences to the so-called human or social sciences and of explanation (*erklärung*) to understanding (*verstehen*). In recent years a rash of texts have appeared advocating the rejection of phenomenology: Penner's (1989) turn to structuralism is accomplished through the destruction of phenomenology on scientific (positivistic) grounds; Lawson and McCauley's (1990) critique of phenomenologists such as Rudolf Otto and Mircea Eliade as "anti-scientific" (1990, 14) provides an opening to argue for a cognitive approach to religion (or at least religious ritual); Fitzgerald's claim that "there has never been a pure, disinterested scholarship in the field of religion" (2000, 39) leads him to anthropology and cultural studies while McCutcheon's (1997) advocacy of "naturalism" likewise proceeds from within the opposition characterized by Paul Ricoeur as a contrast between "interpretation... conceived as the unmasking, demystification or reduction of illusions" and "interpretation conceived as the recollection or restoration of meaning" (1970, 9). However, to argue against phenomenology as unscientific is really to miss the point—after-all, "a traditional logical positivist could agree with most of the assertions being made by contemporary... phenomenologists of religion" (Penner 1989, 32). The claim that religion is *sui generis* is an attempt to clearly delineate an object or specific class of facts for analysis, a strategy also employed by Durkheim in his attempt to define social facts (1982, 54); *epoché* is a commitment to neutrality and value-free description and that facts and values should be strictly separated, a *sine qua non* of positivist science; empathy and the imaginative accessing of an other's mental life is central to Geertz' formulation of anthropology

(1983) and, moreover, to Tylor's reconstruction of the origins of religion (1903, 428), a point which demonstrates that there is no necessary link between empathic liason and interpretive charity. In other words, when the critique of phenomenology proceeds via the invocation of "proper science" (i.e., "value-neutral" research) as a justification for a shift away from phenomenology to cultural studies, anthropology or, indeed, structuralism, we should at all times be aware that the phenomenology of religion is not a crypto-theology as it is sometimes presented, but is part of that vital body of thinking known in the jargon as "social theory" and, moreover the very idea that fact and value can be separated is perhaps the greatest myth—deceit, even—of the Enlightenment tradition. What we should examine, then, are the discursive strategies deployed by phenomenologists to authorize their approach to religion over and above all others. McCutcheon's (1997) archaeology of the discourse of *sui generis* religion is a very useful move in this direction, and it seems to me that the critical blindspot of the phenomenology of religion lies precisely in its inability—even refusal—to question its own knowledge practices and to see itself and its operational concepts in a historical and inter-disciplinary framework.

At this point, a number of perhaps counter-intuitive similarities between structuralism and the phenomenology of religion become visible. First, we might take Lévi-Strauss' approach to myth. Myths, for Lévi-Strauss, constitute their own context—they are a phenomenon *sui generis*. As we have seen, by framing myths this way, Lévi-Strauss feels able to disarticulate them from any socio-historical or political context. Secondly, we might consider Lévi-Strauss' approach to religion (albeit as a mode of thought) and his attempts to represent religion beyond the confines of that ethnocentrism typical of early anthropologists wedded to the evolutionary view of human development, and his commitment to try to understand religion or religious thought both from the inside and the outside. If we are to remark on how this structuralist *epoché* is over-written by Lévi-Strauss in numerous political writings—particularly his uncritical nostalgia for societies without either writing or history—we should note just how similar in form this strategic essentialism is when compared with that developed and elaborated by Mircea Eliade in his own voluminous writings (Eliade 1959, 1969). Although, then, Lévi-Strauss frequently authorizes the structuralist approach via appeals to science, this indeed only serves to blur similarities at a certain level between structuralism and the phenomenology of religion both of which make appeals to value-neutrality to legitimize their respective methods while at the same time smuggling in, through the back door, a veritable cacophony of prior hypotheses and value-saturated assumptions and presuppositions. Thirdly, then, we should

---

Structuralism and phenomenology compared

- Structuralism and phenomenology are conventionally represented as standing at opposite poles of the understanding : explanation continuum. Yet both specify myths as *sui generis*, both make appeals to value-neutrality and both claim to "see" phenomena from the "inside."
- Both also over-write their claims to value-neutrality with critiques of "the West."
- Both also authorize an anonymous and un-locatable knowing subject and are therefore unable to critically reflect on the historicity of their theories and methods.

---

note that structuralism, like the phenomenology of religion, is incapable of reflexively enquiring into the historicity of its own concepts and methods. As Tilley notes, "Lévi-Strauss cannot reflect on the origins of his theories nor relate them to the sets of historical and social circumstances in which he finds himself" (Tilley 1990, 58). These words could equally have been written by McCutcheon in his critique of Eliade.

One apparently fundamental difference between the two approaches lies in their respective views regarding the subject. Flood's (1999) critique of phenomenology and advocacy of "dialogism" turns on an opposition between subject-centred reason for which reason is a tool for mapping and naming objects, and situated co-subjects embedded in the very world(s) they seek to explain or understand. On this analysis, the phenomenology of religion authorizes a particular kind of knowing subject that writes from nowhere with the assurance and calm eye and hand of one whose objectivity is not and never has been in question. Oddly, although structuralism is associated with slogans such as the death of the subject, the question remains as to precisely which subject it is that has been terminated, for Lévi-Strauss seems for the most part able to write from a vantage-point as remote as any occupied by our putative phenomenologist of religion.

If, then, structuralism and phenomenology seem so close, why is it and how is it that in debates about theory and method in the study of religions, they are conventionally represented as occupying opposite ends of the explanation : understanding continuum? The answer to this question lies in the realization that theorizing about theory requires antagonistic thinking: phenomenology needs reductionists in order to really be phenomenology. In truth, however, we should regard the terrain on which the arguments about theory and method have tarried back and forth as a wasteland, scarred and in ruins. The real difference between structuralism and the phenomenology of religion lies in their respective (ideological) appeals for authority and legitimacy: phenomenology to pure vision, pure description and pure representation and structuralism to binary systems, linguistics-as-science, and an *über*-theory for which cultures are kaleidoscopic trans-formations of the mind and which as such envisions mind coming to know itself (though without ever enquiring into the socio-historical specificity of the category "mind"). After post-modernity, we might permit ourselves a wry smile that so much could have been hoped for. We incredulous ones do not and cannot believe.

Bibliography

Adorno, T. and Horkheimer, M. 1944. The Culture Industry: Enlightenment as Mass Deception. In *Dialectic of Enlightenment.* trans. J. Cumming, 120–167. New York: Continuum.

Althusser, L. 2005. *For Marx.* Trans. B. Brewster. London and New York: Verso.

Anderson, B. 1991. *Imagined Communities: Reflections on the Origins and Spread of Nationalism.* London and New York: Verso.

Appadurai, A. 1996. *Modernity at Large: Cultural Dimensions of Globalization.* Minneapolis: University of Minnesota Press.

Asad, T. 1983. Anthropological Conceptions of Religion: Reflections on Geertz. *Man.* 18(3): 237–259.

Badcock, C. R. 1975. *Lévi-Strauss: Structuralism and Sociological Theory.* London: Hutchinson.

Barthes, R. 1977. The Death of the Author. In *Image Music Text,* trans. S. Heath, 142–148. London: Fontana Press.

Bauman, Z. 1999. *Culture as Praxis.* London: Sage.

Best, S. and Kellner, D. 1991. *Postmodern Theory: Critical Interrogations.* London: Macmillan.

Brickman, C. 2003. *Aboriginal Populations in the Mind: Race and Primitivity in Psychoanalysis.* New York: Columbia University Press.

Burridge, K.O.L. 2004. Lévi-Strauss and Myth. In *The Structural Study of Myth and Totemism,* ed. E. Leach, 91–115. London and New York: Routledge.

Callinicos, A. 1999. *Social Theory: An Historical Introduction.* Cambridge: Polity Press.

Capps, W.H. 1995. *Religious Studies: The Making of a Discipline.* Minneapolis, MN: Fortress Press.

Caws, P. 1970. What is Structuralism? In *Claude Lévi-Strauss: The Anthropologist as Hero,* eds. E.N. Hayes and T. Hayes, 197–214. Cambridge, MA and London: MIT Press.

Clarke, J.J. 1997. *Oriental Enlightenment: The Encounter Between Asian and Western Thought*. London and New York: Routledge.

Clastres, P. 1994a. Archeology of Violence: War in Primitive Societies. In *Archeology of Violence,* trans. J. Herman, 139–167. New York: Semiotext(e).

———. 1994b. Marxists and their Anthropology. In *Archeology of Violence,* trans. J. Herman, 127–138. New York: Semiotext(e).

Clifford, J. 1986. Introduction: Partial Truths. In *Writing Culture: The Poetics and Politics of Ethnography,* eds. J. Clifford and G.E. Marcus, 1–26. Berkeley: University of California Press.

Connolly, P., ed. 1999. *Approaches to the Study of Religion*. London and New York: Cassell.

Deliège, R. 2004. *Lévi-Strauss Today: An Introduction to Structural Anthropology*. Trans. N. Scott. Oxford and New York: Berg.

Derrida, J. 1997. *Of Grammatology*. Trans. G.C. Spivak. Baltimore, MD and London: The John Hopkins University Press.

———. 2002. Structure, Sign and Play in the Discourse of the Human Sciences. In *Writing and Difference,* trans. A. Bass, 351–370. London and New York: Routledge.

———. 2004. Plato's Pharmacy. In *Dissemination,* trans. B. Johnson, 67–186. London and New York: Continuum.

Douglas, M. 2004. The Meaning of Myth, with Special Reference to "La Geste d'Asdiwal." In *The Structural Study of Myth and Totemism,* ed. E. Leach, 49–69. London and New York: Routledge.

Dreyfus, H.L. and Rabinow, P. 1983. *Michel Foucault: Beyond Structuralism and Hermeneutics*. Chicago, IL: University of Chicago Press.

Dumont, L. 1980. *Homo Hierarchicus: The Caste System and its Implications*. Trans. M. Sainsbury, L. Dumont and B. Gulati. Chicago, IL and London: Chicago University Press.

Durkheim, E. 1982. *The Rules of Sociological Method*. Ed. S. Lukes, trans. W.D. Halls. London: MacMillan.

Eliade, M. 1959. *The Sacred and the Profane: The Nature of Religion*. New York: Harcourt Brace Jovanovich.

———. 1969. *The Quest: History and Meaning in Religion*. Chicago, IL: University of Chicago.

Ellwood, R. 1999. *The Politics of Myth: A Study of C.G. Jung, Mircea Eliade and Joseph Campbell*. Albany: State University of New York Press.

Endicott, K.M. 1970. *An Analysis of Malay Magic*. Oxford: Clarendon Press.

Evans-Pritchard, E.E. 1965. *Theories of Primitive Religion*. Oxford: Clarendon Press.

Fardon, R. 1990. General Introduction: Localizing Strategies: The Regionalization of Ethnographic Accounts. In *Localizing Strategies: Regional Traditions of Ethnographic Writing,* ed. R. Fardon, 1–35. Edinburgh: Scottish Academic Press.

Fitzgerald, T. 2000. *The Ideology of Religious Studies*. New York and Oxford: Oxford University Press.

Flood, G. 1999. *Beyond Phenomenology: Rethinking the Study of Religion*. London and New York: Cassell.

Fox, R. 2004. *Totem and Taboo* Reconsidered. In *The Structural Study of Myth and Totemism,* ed. E. Leach, 161–178. London and New York: Routledge.

Foucault, M. 1979. *Discipline and Punish: The Birth of the Prison*. Trans. A. Sheridan. Harmondsworth: Penguin.

———. 1992. *The Order of Things: An Archaeology of the Human Sciences*. London and New York: Routledge.

Frazer, J.G. 1910. *Totemism and Exogamy: A Treatise on Certain Early Forms of Superstition and Society, Vol. 1*. London: Macmillan.

———. 1991. *The Golden Bough: A Study in Magic and Religion*. London: Papermac.

Freud, S. 1991. Group Psychology and the Analysis of the Ego. In *Civilization, Society and Religion,* ed. A. Dickson, 91–178. Harmondsworth: Penguin.

———. 2003. *Totem and Taboo: Some Points of Agreement Between the Mental Lives of Savages and Neurotics*. Trans. J. Strachey. London and New York: Routledge.

Gadamer, H-G. 2004. *Truth and Method*. Trans. J. Weinsheimer and D.G. Marshall. London and New York: Continuum.

Geertz, C. 1973. *The Interpretation of Cultures*. New York: Basic Books.

———. 1983. "From The Native's Point of View:" On the Nature of Anthropological Understanding. In *Local Knowledge: Further Essays in Interpretive Anthropology*, 55–70. New York: Basic Books.

Gellner, E. 1986. *Relativism and the Social Sciences*. Cambridge: Cambridge University Press.

———. 1992. *Postmodernism, Reason and Religion*. London and New York: Routledge.

Gupta, A. and Ferguson, J., eds. 2001. *Culture, Power, Place: Explorations in Critical Anthropology*. Durham, NC: Duke University Press.

Gramont, de S. 1970. There are no Superior Societies. In *Claude Lévi-Strauss: The Anthropologist as Hero,* eds. E.N. Hayes and T. Hayes, 3–21. Cambridge, MA and London: M.I.T. Press.

Habermas, J. 2002. An Alternative Way Out of the Philosophy of the Subject: Communicative versus Subject-Centred Reason. In *The Philosophical Discourse of Modernity,* trans. F. Lawrence, 294–326. Cambridge: Polity Press.

Hamilton, M. 2001. *The Sociology of Religion.* London and New York: Routledge.

Haraway, D.J. 1991. Situated Knowledges: The Science Question in Feminism and the Privilege of Partial Perspective. In *Simians, Cyborgs, and Women: The Reinvention of Nature,* 183–201. London: Free Association Books.

Hawkes, T. 1983. *Structuralism and Semiotics.* London: Methuen and Co.

Held, D. 1985. Introduction: Central Perspectives on the Modern State. In *States and Societies,* eds. D. Held, James Anderson, Bram Gieben, Stuart Hall, Laurence Harris, Paul Lewis, Noel Parker and Ben Turok, 1–55. Oxford: Blackwell.

Hénaff, M. 1998. *Claude Lévi-Strauss and the Making of Structural Anthropology.* Trans. M. Baker. Minneapolis and London: University of Minnesota Press.

Hobbes, T. 1985. Leviathan. in *States and Societies,* eds. D. Held, James Anderson, Bram Gieben, Stuart Hall, Laurence Harris, Paul Lewis, Noel Parker and Ben Turok, 68–71. Oxford: Blackwell.

Hoy, D.C. 1994. Introduction. In *Foucault: A Critical Reader,* ed. D.C. Hoy, 1–25. Oxford: Blackwell.

Jackson, P. A. 2002. Thai Buddhist Identity: Debates on the *Traiphum Phra Ruang.* In *National Identity and its Defenders: Thailand Today,* ed. C.J. Reynolds, 155–188. Chiang Mai: Silkworm Books.

Jakobson, R. and Halle, M. 1956. *Fundamentals of Language.* The Hague: Mouton and Co.

Jameson, F. 1972. *The Prison-House of Language: A Critical Account of Structuralism and Russian Formalism.* Princeton, NJ: Princeton University Press.

Jenks, C. 2003. *Transgression.* London and New York: Routledge.

Johnson, C. 2003. *Claude Lévi-Strauss: The Formative Years.* Cambridge: Cambridge University Press.

Jones, R.A. 2005. *The Secret of the Totem: Religion and Society from McLennan to Freud.* New York: Columbia University Press.

Keyes, C.F. 1989. *Thailand: Buddhist Kingdom as Modern Nation-State.* Bangkok: Duang Kamol.

King, R. 1999. *Orientalism and Religion: Post-Colonial Theory, India and the Mystic East.* London and New York: Routledge.

King, V.T. and Wilder, W.D. 2003. *The Modern Anthropology of South-East Asia.* London and New York: Routledge Curzon.

Kuhn, T. 1970. *The Structure of Scientific Revolutions.* Chicago, IL and London: University of Chicago Press.

Kunin, S.D. 2003. *Religion: The Modern Theories.* Baltimore, MD and London: John Hopkins University Press.

Lacan, J. 1989. *Écrits: A Selection.* Trans. A Sheridan. London and New York: Routledge.

Lawson, E.T. and McCauley, R.N. 1990. *Rethinking Religion: Connecting Cognition and Culture.* Cambridge: Cambridge University Press.

Leach, E.R. 1970a. Brain-twister. In *Claude Lévi-Strauss: The Anthropologist as Hero,* eds. E.N. Hayes and T. Hayes, 123–132. Cambridge, MA and London: MIT Press.

———. 1970b. Lévi-Strauss in the Garden of Eden: An Examination of Some Recent Developments in the Analysis of Myth. In *Claude Lévi-Strauss: The Anthropologist as Hero,* eds. E.N. Hayes and T. Hayes, 47–60. Cambridge, MA and London: MIT Press.

———. 1974. *Claude Lévi-Strauss.* New York: The Viking Press.

Lévi-Strauss, C. 1966. *The Savage Mind.* London: Weidenfeld and Nicolson.

———. 1969. *The Elementary Structures of Kinship.* Trans. J.H. Bell, J.R. von Sturmer and R. Needham. London: Eyre and Spottiswoode.

———. 1981. *The Naked Man: Introduction to a Science of Mythology 4.* Trans. J. and D. Weightman. London: Cape.

———. 1985a. Cross-Readings. In *The View from Afar,* trans. J. Neugroschel and P. Hoss, 73–87. Harmondsworth: Penguin.

———. 1985b. The Family. In *The View from Afar,* trans. J. Neugroschel and P. Hoss, 39–62. Harmondsworth: Penguin.

———. 1985c. The Anthropologist and the Human Condition. In *The View from Afar,* trans. J. Neugroschel and P. Hoss, 25–36. Harmondsworth: Penguin.

———. 1985d. The Lessons of Linguistics. In *The View from Afar,* trans. J. Neugroschel and P. Hoss, 138–147. Harmondsworth: Penguin.

———. 1985e. Race and Culture. In *The View from Afar,* trans. J. Neugroschel and P. Hoss, 3–24. Harmondsworth: Penguin.

———. 1985f. Reflections on Liberty. In *The View from Afar,* trans. J. Neugroschel and P. Hoss, 279–288. Harmondsworth: Penguin.

———. 1991. *Totemism.* Trans. R. Needham. London: Merlin Press.

———. 1992a. *Tristes Tropiques.* Trans. J. and D. Weightman. Harmondsworth: Penguin.

———. 1992b. *The Raw and the Cooked: Introduction to a Science of Mythology 1,* trans. J. and D. Weightman. Harmondsworth: Penguin.

———. 1993a. Structural Analysis in Linguistics and in Anthropology. In *Structural Anthropology Volume 1,* trans. C. Jocobson and B.G. Schoepf, 31–54. Harmondsworth: Penguin.

———. 1993b. Linguistics and Anthropology. In *Structural Anthropology Volume 1,* trans. C. Jocobson and B.G. Schoepf,67–80. Harmondsworth: Penguin.

———. 1993c. Postscript to Chapters III and IV. In *Structural Anthropology,* vol. 1, trans. C. Jocobson and B.G. Schoepf, 81–97. Harmondsworth: Penguin.

———. 1993d. Introduction: History and Anthropology. In *Structural Anthropology,* vol. 1, trans. C. Jocobson and B.G. Schoepf, 1–27. Harmondsworth: Penguin.

———. 1993e. Language and the Analysis of Social Laws. In *Structural Anthropology,* vol. 1, trans. C. Jocobson and B.G. Schoepf, 55–66. Harmondsworth: Penguin.

———. 1993f. The Place of Anthropology in the Social Sciences and Problems Raised in Teaching It. In *Structural Anthropology,* vol. 1, trans. C. Jocobson and B.G. Schoepf, 346–381. Harmondsworth: Penguin.

———. 1993g. The Structural Study of Myth. In *Structural Anthropology,* vol. 1, trans. C. Jocobson and B.G. Schoepf, 206–231. Harmondsworth: Penguin.

———. 1993h. The Sorcerer and his Magic. In *Structural Anthropology,* vol. 1, trans. C. Jocobson and B.G. Schoepf, 167–185. Harmondsworth: Penguin.

———. 1993i. The Effectiveness of Symbols. In *Structural Anthropology,* vol. 1, trans. C. Jocobson and B.G. Schoepf, 186–205. Harmondsworth: Penguin.

———. 1994a. Race and History. In *Structural Anthropology,* vol. 2, trans. M. Layton, 323–362. Harmondsworth: Penguin.

———. 1994b. Jean-Jacques Rousseau, Founder of the Sciences of Man. In *Structural Anthropology,* vol. 2, trans. M. Layton, 33–43. Harmondsworth: Penguin.

————. 1994c. Answers to Some Investigations. In *Structural Anthropology,* vol. 2, trans. M. Layton, 271–287. Harmondsworth: Penguin.

————. 1994d. The Scope of Anthropology. In *Structural Anthropology,* vol. 2, trans. M. Layton, 3–32. Harmondsworth: Penguin.

————. 1994e. The Story of Asdiwal. In *Structural Anthropology,* vol. 2, trans. M. Layton, 146–197. Harmondsworth: Penguin.

————. 1994f. Comparative Religion of Nonliterate Peoples. In *Structural Anthropology,* vol. 2, trans. M. Layton, 60–67. Harmondsworth: Penguin.

————. 1994g. Cultural Discontinuity and Economic and Social Development. In *Structural Anthropology,* vol. 2, trans. M. Layton, 312–322. Harmondsworth: Penguin.

————. 2001. *Myth and Meaning.* London and New York: Routledge.

Lévi -Strauss, C. and Eribon, D. 1991. *Conversations with Claude Lévi-Strauss.* Trans. P. Wissing. Chicago, IL and London: The University of Chicago Press.

Malinowski, B. 1984a. Magic, Science and Religion. In *Magic, Science and Religion and Other Essays*, 17–92. Westport, CT: Greenwood Press.

————. 1984b. Myth in Primitive Psychology. In *Magic, Science and Religion and Other Essays*, 93–148. Westport, CT: Greenwood Press.

Marx, K. 1992. *Karl Marx: Early Writings.* Trans. R. Livingstone and G. Benton. Harmondsworth: Penguin.

Mauss, M. 1954. *The Gift: Forms and Functions of Exchange in Archaic Societies.* Trans. I. Cunnison. London: Cohen and West Ltd.

Maybury-Lewis, D. 1970. Science or Bricolage? In *Claude Lévi-Strauss: The Anthropologist as Hero,* eds. E.N. Hayes and T. Hayes, 150–163. Cambridge, MA and London: MIT Press.

Marcuse, H. 1964. *One-Dimensional Man.* London: Sphere.

McCutcheon, R.T. 1997. *Manufacturing Religion: The Discourse on Sui Generis Religion and the Politics of Nostalgia.* New York and Oxford: Oxford University Press.

McKinnon, S. 2001. The Economies in Kinship and the Paternity of Culture: Origin Stories in Kinship Theory. In *Relative Values: Reconfiguring Kinship Studies,* eds. S. Franklin and S. McKinnon, 277–301. Durham, NC and London: Duke University Press.

McLuhan, M. 2004. *Understanding Media.* London and New York: Routledge.

Mendelson, E. M. 2004. The "Uninvited Guest": Ancilla to Lévi-Strauss on Totemism and Primitive Thought. In *The Structural Study of Myth and Totemism,* ed. E. Leach, 119–139. London and New York: Routledge.

Merquior, J. G, 1988. *From Prague to Paris: A Critique of Structuralist and Post-Structuralist Thought.* London and New York: Verso.

Moran, D. 2000. *Introduction to Phenomenology.* London and New York: Routledge.

Morris, B. 1987. *Anthropological Studies of Religion: An Introductory Text.* Cambridge: Cambridge University Press.

Needham, R. 1962. *Structure and Sentiment: A Test Case in Social Anthropology.* Chicago, IL and London: University of Chicago Press.

——. 1971. *Rethinking Kinship and Marriage.* London: Tavistock.

Neu, J. 1975. Lévi-Strauss on Shamanism. *Man.* 10(2): 285–292.

Otto, R. 1928. *The Idea of the Holy.* Trans. J.W. Harvey. Oxford: Oxford University Press.

Pace, D. 1986. *Claude Lévi-Strauss: The Bearer of Ashes.* London: Ark Paperbacks.

Pals, D. 2006. *Eight Theories of Religion.* Oxford: Oxford University Press.

Penner, H. H. 1989. *Impasse and Resolution: A Critique of the Study of Religion.* New York: Lang.

Radcliffe-Brown, A.R. 1958. The Comparative Method in Social Anthropology. In *Method in Social Anthropology,* ed. M.N. Srinivas, 108–129. Chicago, IL and London: University of Chicago Press.

——. 1965. The Sociological Theory of Totemism. In *Structure and Function in Primitive Society,* 117–132. New York: The Free Press.

Ricoeur, P. 1970. *Freud and Philosophy: An Essay in Interpretation.* Trans. D. Savage. New Haven, CT: Yale University Press.

——. 1974. The Hermeneutics of Symbols and Philosophical Reflection: II. In *The Conflict of Interpretations*, 315–334. Evanston, IL: Northwestern University Press.

——. 2004. Structure and Hermeneutics. In *The Conflict of Interpretations: Essays in Hermeneutics*, 27–60. London and New York: Continuum.

Said, E. 1995. *Orientalism: Western Conceptions of the Orient.* Harmondsworth: Penguin.

Segal, R.A. 1999. *Theorizing About Myth*. Amhurst: University of Massachusetts Press.

———. 2004. *Myth: A Very Short Introduction*. Oxford: Oxford University Press.

Sharpe, E.J. 1986. *Comparative Religion: A History*. London: Duckworth.

Sontag, S. 1970. The Anthropologist as Hero. In *Claude Lévi-Strauss: The Anthropologist as Hero*, eds. E.N. Hayes and T. Hayes, 184–196. Cambridge, MA and London: MIT Press.

Steiner, G. 1970. Orpheus with his Myths. In *Claude Lévi-Strauss: The Anthropologist as Hero*, eds. E.N. Hayes and T. Hayes, 170–183. Cambridge, MA and London: MIT Press.

Strenski, I. 1987. *Four Theories of Myth in Twentieth-Century History: Cassirer, Eliade, Lévi-Strauss and Malinowski*. London: Macmillan.

Sturrock, J. 1993. *Structuralism*. London: Fontana Press.

Sukatipan, S. 1995. Thailand: The Evolution of Legitimacy. In *Political Legitimacy in Southeast Asia: The Quest for Moral Authority*, ed. M. Alagappa, 193–223. Stanford, CA: Stanford University Press.

Tambiah, S.J. 1970. *Buddhism and the Spirit Cults in North-East Thailand*. Cambridge: Cambridge University Press.

Thompson, K. (ed). 2004. *Readings from Emile Durkheim*. London and New York: Routledge.

Tilley, C. 1990. Claude Lévi-Strauss: Structuralism and Beyond. In *Reading Material Culture: Structuralism, Hermeneutics and Post-Structuralism*, ed. C. Tilley, 3–81. Oxford: Basil Blackwell.

Turner, B.S. 1991. *Religion and Social Theory*. London: Sage.

Tylor, E.B. 1903. *Primitive Culture: Researches into the Development of Mythology, Philosophy, Religion, Language, Art and Custom*. London: John Murray.

Worsley, P. 2004. Groote Eylandt Totemism and *Le Totemisme Aujourd'hui*. in *The Structural Study of Myth and Totemism*, ed. E. Leach, 141–159. London and New York: Routledge.

Zimmerman, R.L. 1970. Lévi-Strauss and the Primitive. In *Claude Lévi-Strauss: The Anthropologist as Hero*, eds. E.N. Hayes and T. Hayes, 215–234. Cambridge, MA and London: MIT Press.

Index

A

aborigines, Australian, 47
  Arunta, 43
  Murngin, 30
abreaction, psychoanalytic, 82
Adorno, Theodor, 93
Althusser, Louis, 5, 24, 25, 26
Andaman Islanders, 39
Anderson, Benedict, 91, 92
animism, 48–49
anthropology
  critiqued by Lévi-Strauss, 21
  cultural preservation and, 95
  functionalist, 20
  mathematics and, 30
  meaning and, 69
  phenomenology and, 101
  Saussure and, 15
  structural linguistics and, 9, 11,
    17–18, 24, 68, 76, 97
  perspective of, 93–94
  pre-structuralist, 19–20
  science and, 22, 23, 37
  social reform and, 96
  See also culture; kinship; myth; sha-
    manism; totemism
anti-humanism, 11, 96
aphasia, 15
art
  Caduveo, 82–83
  as language, 18
  See also music
Arunta (Australian aborigines), 43
asceticism, 5, 24, 47
Asdiwal. *See* "Story of Asdiwal, The"
  (Lévi-Strauss)
authorship, vii–viii, 70–71, 86
  See also texts

B

Babeuf, Gracchus, 1
Badcock, C. R., 19
Bastide, Roger, 2
Bauman, Zygmunt, 20
Benveniste, Emile, 24
Bergson, Henri, 51–52
Best, Steven, 25
binary oppositions
  cultural variation and, 11, 92
  myth and, 62–63, 64, 65
  la pensée sauvage and, 76
  totemism and, 51–52
Boas, Franz, 2, 24
Bororo (Amerindian group), 2, 65
Brickman, Celia, 49–50
bricolage, 50, 75–76, 77, 78
Buddhism, 97–98
Burridge, Ken O.L., 57

C

Caduveo (Amerindian tribe), 2, 77,
  82–83
Capps, Walter H., ix
caste, 5, 24, 82–83, 89
childhood, 48–49
Christianity, 44
clans, 44, 45, 46
  See also kinship
classification, systems of
  culture and, 11, 15, 92
  myth and, 76
  totemism and, 43, 50, 76
Clastres, Pierre, 33, 35–37, 67
Comte, Auguste, 76
Connolly, Peter, ix
consciousness, collective, 13, 77, 79
  See also mind

Printed in the United States
212906BV00002B/4/P

9 781845 532789

Series Editor: Steven Engler
Mount Royal College, Canada

Lévi-Strauss on Religion

Claude Lévi-Strauss and the style of thinking known as "structuralism" with which his work is conventionally associated is widely recognized as having made a seminal contribution to the discipline of anthropology. More generally, his writings register the turn to language in social theory in the 1960s, and are marked by the influence of Kant, Rousseau, Saussurian linguistics, Marx and Freud. In turn, Lévi-Strauss is recognized as having been a key influence on thinkers such as Althusser, Lacan, Foucault and Derrida. This volume seeks to address a key gap in the burgeoning secondary literature about Lévi-Strauss: his importance to the study of religions. This volume pays particular attention to Lévi-Strauss' writings on totemism, myth and "la pensée sauvage" situating these writings both in terms of previous theories of religion and in terms of the wider influences that informed his work.

This volume provides an accessible and comprehensive overview of Lévi-Strauss' life and work, the thinkers and theories that informed his writings, and his contribution to the study of religions.

Paul-François Tremlett is a Research Associate at the School of Oriental and African Studies and a Visiting Lecturer at the Institute of Ismaili Studies in London. He has published essays on theory and method in the study of religions, on religion and nationalism and religion and masculinity in the Philippines and on the anthropology of religion on Taiwan. He is co-editor of a volume of essays about Taiwan entitled *Re-Writing Culture: Perspectives via Taiwan* (Routledge, 2008) and author of *Religion and the Discourse on Modernity* (Continuum, 2008).

Printed in Great Britain
ISBN 978-1-84553-278-9

www.equinoxpub.com

9 781845 532789